■ This book grows out of a study of work with street groups that was made possible by a grant recommended by the Duncan Russell Memorial Delinquency Committee of the United Community Services of Metropolitan Boston, and provided by the Permanent Charity Fund of Boston. ■

# Youth
## on the Streets

WORK WITH

ALIENATED YOUTH GROUPS

*Saul Bernstein*

ASSOCIATION PRESS    NEW YORK

A BOOK IS GENERATED out of the hopes of the author. I will state mine frankly. This book is meant to arouse people to a better understanding of how life looks and feels to our alienated youth in large cities, to a recognition of the extent and seriousness of the problems they face, and to the inadequacy of the resources which communities provide for them.

# Preface

It also represents the fulfillment of promises made to young people during those haunting experiences in the course of this assignment when I met with them to talk over their problems, to tell the world about them.

It is also a response to the men and women who are dedicating themselves to staggering and frequently discouraging problems while, as agency and community representatives, they spend their days, evenings, sometimes even nights on the streets working with these volatile adolescents, talking with their families, sitting with them in court, trying to help them with school and jobs. Even as they poured out their stories of effort and frustration, they expressed the hope that in some way the knowledge gained in my visits to other cities with similar problems would be made available to them.

My profound gratitude for unstinting cooperation goes to them, to their supervisors and agency executives, to judges, probation officers, police, school officials and others who gave so generously of their time and interest.

I would also like to extend my thanks to the Permanent Charity Fund of Boston and the Duncan Russell Memorial Delinquency Committee of the United Community Services of Metropolitan Boston for the grant which made this venture possible, and to Boston University and Dean John McDowell of the School of Social Work for facilitating a sabbatical leave.

This book is the product of my experiences on the firing line of

one of the most serious sets of problems facing our nation, experiences at once stirring and sobering, carrying with them a sense of almost desperate urgency. Solutions are being sought, but on far too limited a scale. I hope that this sense of urgency will communicate itself to others, particularly to those in positions to influence public policy. It is my aim that from this distillation of the experiences and ideas of many people who are working with alienated youth groups, readers will be inspired to act to bring about innovations with regard to services and programs, as well as desperately needed changes in the larger socio-economic scene, for a more effective assault on the devastating problems facing, and in some instances even destroying, so many of our youth.

SAUL BERNSTEIN

Boston University

THIS BOOK is about youth groups at the social and economic bottom of our society, disturbingly alienated from the middle-class community. Most of them have come from minority backgrounds, such as Negro, Mexican-American, Puerto Rican and others. What are they doing, feeling and thinking? What are the patterns of their

# Introduction

groupings and with what bearing on delinquency? How do life and the future look to them? These are major questions to which the book is addressed.

What explanations or theories help us to understand and work with these young people? Is any one of the popular theories adequate to explain the massive and complex problems faced by disinherited youth? What socio-economic conditions deeply and pervasively affect their lives and their perceptions of the future? Answers to these questions are sought in the book.

Streetwork (sometimes called "detached group work," "area youth work," etc.) has been developed as an approach specifically designed for alienated and sublower-class youth groups. What is solidly known about its concepts and methods; what are the gaps? What can be expected in the way of realistic accomplishments; where does the approach run into the limits of its effectiveness? What is the role of streetwork in relation to a wide range of community services, to the families and neighborhoods of the youth? These are major concerns of chapters which follow.

The streetworker is unusual among people who provide community services. What are his characteristics and what are the sources of strength and competence which motivate and guide him? Where does he stand in the prestige hierarchy? What are his problems and what needs to be done to solve them?

An increasing amount of research is being devoted to alienated youth groups. How helpful is it to the practitioner and in what ways does it forward or retard his efforts? What are some of the usable

findings from research? How can the practitioner participate more productively and cooperatively in research? Are there specific problems which call urgently for research attention?

The blockage of educational, vocational and social opportunities for sublower-class youth is getting increasing attention not only as a cause of delinquency but also as a grave source of social stratification and injustice. How do those working with such youth groups assess these obstacles to upward movement? To what resources should we look to provide for the opening of doors for masses of youth whose horizons are so limited? To these questions, too, the book is devoted.

The approach followed by the writer needs to be shared with the reader. Nine cities (Chicago, Cleveland, Los Angeles, San Francisco, Detroit, New York, Philadelphia, Washington and Boston) were visited because 1) they had substantial numbers of hostile youth groups, and 2) long experience was available in working with them. Material from other cities was consulted. A list of questions (Appendix B) was prepared and pre-tested. They provided the basis for many interviews with streetworkers and their supervisors and executives. In addition, less structured interviews were held with judges, police officials, probation officers, psychiatrists, school officials, researchers and others. Central in the enterprise were discussions with youth groups and with a few of their parents.

Studies, reports, proposals and the general literature were consulted in the attempt to reach a rounded view of a mountainous set of problems. Inevitably, the values, commitments and biases of the writer have affected the chapters which follow. The question of objectivity is old and difficult. Rather than attempt to disguise or minimize his values, the writer hopes that he makes them clear as the chapters unfold and that he handles them with sufficient discipline so that the data are fully respected.

\*      \*      \*

Some distance between adolescents and adults may have been characteristic of many societies in history. A thesis of this book is that the gap has become alarmingly great between youth at the bottom, the sublower class, and the respectable adult community, so great that it threatens to become the most important domestic

problem in the United States. How these adolescents can fit into the mainstream of healthy and productive adulthood is far from clear. Also disturbing is the seeming lack of awareness of the scope and seriousness of the problem on the part of both the general public and people in positions to formulate policy. This book is devoted to spelling out the problem and to suggestions of ways to cope with it.

# Contents

Leadership

Kinds of Delinquent Behavior

Rumbles and Other Kinds of Fighting

Dress

Larger Movements

Special Problems

A. Drugs

B. Drinking

C. Sex and Unmarried Mothers

D. Residuals

Values and Psychological Characteristics

Patterns of Organization and Sources of Funds

A. City-Wide Public Agencies

B. Combined Public and Voluntary Sources of Funds

C. Voluntary and City-Wide

D. Voluntary—not City-Wide

E. Special Patterns

Comments

Selection of Groups to Be Served

The Contacts

A. Families

B. Schools

C. Securing Psychiatric Help

D. Police

E. Courts and Probation Officers

F. Other Contacts

Problems of Strategy

"THERE IS NOTHING so practical as a good theory" is more than intellectual folklore. Theories may be good or bad, but without them experience cannot be ordered, nor can meanings be derived from it, nor can we find intelligent leverage for effecting social change. The real question is not whether we need theory, but

# theories and Conditions

rather, which ones clarify the situation and give us effective tools for movement toward solutions. Some of the major theories regarding delinquency follow.

### Opportunity-Blockage[1]

Sublower-class and minority group youngsters do not have access to or are not able to utilize, educational, economic and social opportunities to achieve satisfaction and status in the mainstream of legal and generally approved activities. There is often a confluence of home and neighborhood influences with those of institutions representing the community (schools, police, recreation centers) resulting in the perception by the youngsters that the roads to the middle class are blocked. In some cities, it was stated that even illegitimate opportunities have decreased because some racketeers have moved to the suburbs and developed a kind of big-business bureaucracy in which there is little room for the impetuous teenager.

Since the needs to achieve and to have a place under some sort of a sun are as strong as ever, these adolescents turn to opportunities which are available: association with each other, fighting, drinking, sexual activity, car theft, drugs, and the like. The great

[1] See Richard A. Cloward and Lloyd E. Ohlin, *Delinquency and Opportunity* (Glencoe, Illinois: Free Press, 1960).

**15**

energy and aspirations of the adolescent must go somewhere. If they are blocked in desirable directions, others will be found.

This theory has made a great impact; a substantial part of the push in new directions, stimulated by funds from the President's Committee on Delinquency and Youth Crime, is toward the opening up of educational and occupational opportunities. It provides a large and powerful lever for understanding, and doing something about, delinquency. However, it does not in itself account for individual variations. Some youngsters from similarly poor backgrounds do find places on the educational and occupational ladders, and many do not become delinquents. They may need to have unusual strengths and motivations, but they do manage to go over the obstacles. These strengths and motivations must be explained in terms of theory different from the opportunity-blockage position.

### The Cultural Approach[2]

Many lower-class neighborhoods have developed a relatively stable subculture in which forms of criminal and delinquent values and behavior are accepted as norms. As young people grow up, their models, those who set the standards, are set in this illegal pattern, and the pressures to conform to it are great. Support for this theory was advanced by many of the streetworkers interviewed by the writer when they indicated that a major obstacle to the success of their efforts were the contrary standards of many of the neighborhoods in which they worked. These influences placed the worker in a somewhat isolated position in relation to the groups of young people. Certainly a major component in the diagnosing of any such group is the character of the neighborhood in which it lives.

Qualifications of this subcultural approach need to be recognized. The illegal subcultural is never pure. There are always counterforces within individuals who are part of it, as well as in neighborhood people who have more law-abiding standards. Furthermore, the subculture in a large city is not isolated. The larger community influences it in a variety of ways through schools, police, mass media and the like. The reactions to such influences may

---

[2] For proponents of this point of view, see Albert K. Cohen, *Delinquent Boys* (Glencoe, Illinois: Free Press, 1955) and William C. Kvaraceus and Walter B. Miller, *Delinquent Behavior: Culture and the Individual* (National Education Association [Washington, D.C., 1959]).

be largely negative, but they are present and are felt. As was suggested in relation to the opportunity theory, some individuals do not yield to the criminal subculture and they need to be explained.

Originating in the realities of the material included in this theory are special problems facing intervention efforts. We know less about how to change subcultures than we do about influencing individuals, groups and even organizations. A subculture is massive and it has so many dimensions that it is hard to know where, when and how to take hold. Nevertheless, several delinquency control programs are in some respects tackling this problem. Examples are Mobilization for Youth in New York and the Demonstration of Community Action for Youth in the Hough area of Cleveland. In these, as well as in other programs, the approaches are many-sided and it seems to be almost impossible to test solely the culture theory.

### Poverty and Affluence

We are in a strange state of increased affluence existing alongside tremendous poverty. The latter has been given considerable attention in the last few years. Referring to figures from the Bureau of the Census, 1961, Elizabeth Herzog [3] says: "It has . . . been reported that in 1960, almost one fifth of the white and almost half of the nonwhite families [in the United States] had under $3,000 annual money income; while 24% of the nonwhite and 7% of the white fell below $1500." Miss Herzog points out the complexities of making precise estimates of the scope and nature of poverty, but the figures she quotes are brute realities involving millions of people. In the same article, she outlines the findings of various studies:

"Poverty involves under-employment and scattered, irregular, miscellaneous employment often at undesirable occupations; it involves extensive borrowing through formal and informal sources, use of second-hand clothing and furniture, over-crowded dwellings and lack of privacy. The poor have a higher death rate, a lower life expectancy, lower levels of health—physical and mental—and of nutrition, than the prosperous; they depend more on home remedies and folk medicine since medical care is expensive and

---

[3] Elizabeth Herzog, "Some Assumptions about the Poor," *Social Service Review,* December, 1963.

frightening; they are relatively unlikely to be members of labor
unions, political parties, and other organizations; they are more
inclined to excessive drinking and violence than the prosperous."

Miss Herzog goes on to suggest that the fact of poverty is so
powerful in its influence that it may well count more than race,
and negative characteristics often attributed to Negroes probably
are more symptomatic of poverty than of color.

To enable one to grasp more specifically the quality and problems of living in poverty, excerpts about health are offered from
a fact sheet, "Some Health Problems in North Lawndale [Chicago]
Community Area," 1962, prepared by Aaron Spitzer, Welfare
Council of Metropolitan Chicago, and Arthur I. Solomon, Jr., Chicago Youth Centers:

Population—1960—124,937. Predominantly lower-class Negroes.
*Tuberculosis*
  More than one in five people are positive reactors—have been
  infected with TB germs. Less than twenty percent of the resi-
  dents have chest X-rays each year.
*Rat-Control*
  Thirty bitten by rats and mice during 1961. Resident partici-
  pation in a rat-control plan is nonexistent.
*Dental*
  More than eight out of ten children suffer dental decay and
  neglect.
  No dental clinic is available within this area that is open full
  days all year long to attend to the neglect among indigent children and adults.
*Vision*
  One out of every four children has vision below minimum
  standards and needs glasses.
  Over forty percent of the adult population is visually handi-
  capped and needs glasses.
  Pre-school, high school, college and adult age mass vision testing is practically non-existent.
*Illegitimacy*
  1,658 illegitimate births during 1961; thirty-two percent of babies born being illegitimate.

One could go on with the sad facts. Lawndale, to be sure, is extreme, but similar areas exist elsewhere. It is not stretching fact or

reason to associate the stark data on poverty with high delinquency rates.

Poverty has been related to delinquency for a long time, but in the United States and other prosperous countries we have something relatively recent: poverty surrounded by widespread affluence highly visible through the mass media, the prevalence of automobiles and the general nearness of the poor to the products of prosperity.[4] Tension develops between the aspirations created among poor youngsters and their resources for attaining expensive articles through legitimate means. This helps to understand the high incidence of car theft and such a seemingly strange circumstance as the adolescent at the bottom of the socio-economic heap managing to have a suit—often only one—that sells for a higher price than many more affluent people feel they can afford. Whatever the sublower-class youngster may think of middle-class people and their ideas, he likes their attendant rewards.

In the past there was a greater degree of distance, both physical and social, between wealth and poverty, but today's poor may read the same papers, hear the same radio programs, watch the same television shows, and share in vicarious awareness generally the products of affluence. The teenager living in poverty is subjected to appeals to buy as is his middle-class confrere, yet the means to do so legitimately are not available to him. Pressures build up, with counterforces against delinquent behavior often being weak. It is understandable, then, that he frequently succumbs, especially in relation to the theft of property.

To cite factual support for the number of acts against property: the "Juvenile Statistics Report" of the Philadelphia Police Department for 1961 lists a total of 9,011 arrests, of which 1,459 were for burglary, 1,575 for larceny, 800 for auto theft, and 445 for robbery, for a subtotal of 4,279 arrests for crimes involving property, not much under half the total arrests.

Fyvel cites a strange development in Great Britain: as the standard of living of the poor rose in the postwar years, the incidence of delinquency and troublesome gang behavior increased. This would seem to refute the poverty thesis, yet the pressures to own and

---

[4] An exposition of this point of view is found in T. R. Fyvel, *The Troublemakers* (New York: Shocken Books, 1961-62). The book gives an international picture of youth problems.

spend more probably far outstripped the actual increase in income. Furthermore, unlike many middle-class people, the poor are usually not psychologically and socially prepared to be disciplined and prudent in handling money. This is a weakness in any approach to delinquency limited to providing jobs and greater income. The transition from the characteristics of poverty described by Miss Herzog to stable and planned living is more than economic.

The theory that poverty amid affluence produces delinquency is a powerful one, but it poses great difficulties for intervention. Appreciably raising the standard of living of the poor is essential, whether it prevents delinquency or not. Providing more and better jobs, especially for minorities, is a matter of compelling justice. Higher allowances for Public Assistance, Aid to Dependent Children and other forms of subsidy are essential for decent living. Along with these must go a variety of services to be discussed later.

The problem of lessening the impact of visible affluence on the poor is difficult. Advertising and the mass media are part of our society and the poor cannot be placed outside their influence. Perhaps the best hope is that extended and improved community services will help develop the values needed for thoughtful planning, which aim has not been completely achieved by the middle class.

### General Breakdown in Standards[5]

This position extends the subculture thesis to the larger society. It presents the impulse toward acquisition as running wild, not sufficiently inhibited by other values which are publicly professed. Examples are political corruption, sharp practices in business, rigged television programs, exploitation of minorities, misuse of public relations, and many other examples of the sacrifice of integrity for the sake of the "fast buck." Some such actions are done deliberately and consciously; others are part of "the system." In either case, the impact on sublower-class and other youngsters results in a philosophy of "what's in it for me?" and "what's your angle?" The arena is formidably moved beyond criminal, gang and lower-class values to the larger question of what American society regards as "the good life."

[5] See Max Lerner, *America as a Civilization* (New York: Simon & Schuster, 1957), Chapter IX.

A great advantage of this position is that the task of preventing and controlling delinquency is taken out of the false context of good and competent people doing things for and to bad and incompetent others. It poses the moral issues for all of us. It raises delicate questions as to where to place on the scale of ethics the crude delinquencies of the sublower class in comparison with subtler and more complex violations by people in high positions. The integrity of our society is under X-ray and the picture is far from heartening.

The implications for work with delinquents in the context of a breakdown in standards are soul-searching. The youngsters are sophisticated in this area, and reinforcement comes from their own lack of trust in people and society. Therefore, one must be honest with them about dishonesty. In their eyes, the law does not have majesty and those charged with its enforcement are enemies. As one boy put it, the picture of Justice blindfolded tells the story. While recognizing with delinquents that there is some basis for their distrust, the challenge is to convince them that many people are basically honest, that by and large the law is reasonable, and that many police, judges and probation officers *do* care about what happens to them. It is a long, arduous and often discouraging task to learn to believe in human decency in the face of much evidence to the contrary. Hostile, sublower-class youngsters do not respond favorably to pretty speeches. They are reached by concrete evidence in the mainstream of their experience.

The exact relationship between integrity in our society and delinquency is extremely difficult to assess. The connection seems reasonable and might be accepted on that basis, rather than as established by research. Certainly there is much experience with delinquents which shows the negative impact on and destructive use by the youngsters of lack of integrity in people who should be their models, just as the presence of decency, given time, makes itself felt.

### Psychodynamic Theory

This is largely psychoanalytic theory which traces much of delinquency back to failures in family relationships during the early years of childhood, and to continuing family difficulties. Many as-

pects of this theory are well-known, but one point calls for special attention. In going through the stages of individual development, any failure to meet the requirements of each has a cumulative effect, i.e., the person is still struggling with what he should have mastered earlier. This, in turn, interferes with successful social functioning in the present. Significant applications of this idea can be made to delinquents, many of whose levels of socialization and degrees of narcissism and impulse control more nearly resemble those of younger children. Streetworkers gave examples of adolescents in their groups who, when out in the country, rolled down hills and scampered around in a way, again, more characteristic of younger children. There were also instances of childlike fears of bird calls at night, darkness, and areas new to them, not consistent with their ostensible toughness. The sensitive worker should be understanding of this type of behavior, and accept it, although not to the point of stimulating it further.

More generally, psychodynamic theory is helpful in understanding and dealing with: 1) the development of the individual, 2) psychopathology, and 3) family relationships. Care must be used to adapt psychodynamic concepts to specific conditions, such as those in a hostile group of adolescents of sublower-class origins and their environs. Much of their pathology is social, and behavior which might be frowned upon elsewhere is functional for them. Fighting is a good illustration; without it a boy would be lost in relation to his peers and to many adults in his neighborhood. The diagnostic challenge is to sort out what belongs to the mores of the subculture from what is clearly individual pathology.

A sometimes-overlooked contribution of psychodynamic theory is the help it can offer in identifying normal growth needs and understanding the obstacles to movement toward healthy maturity. Delinquents should not be stereotyped or caricatured as a separate human breed. Most, if not all, of them are very much like the rest of us, perhaps even more sensitive, in their feelings, pleasures and pains.

### Rites of Passage

The successful movement from adolescence to adulthood is complex and uneven in our society. In some ways it is eased and made

pleasant for the competent middle-class youngster, who receives much support and has many opportunities for fun during his high school and college years. Even he faces some turbulence, uncertainty and lack of inner assurance. But the sublower-class youngster is much more beset with difficulties in moving toward adulthood. While he experiences some aspects of adolescence and even of adulthood (independence of parents) earlier than his middle-class confrere, other dimensions of adulthood are confused and uncertain. Marriage and a regular income via a job are central goals and yet, increasingly, the route to them has become more education, a prerequisite for a satisfactory job. If he is a school dropout—and many are—the only road may be blocked. After repeated failures in school and much negative feeling about it, he is apt to regard it as hopeless to try to return. Where does this leave him with adulthood? Yet he wants the outlets of grown-ups, such as sexual activity, becoming a parent, drinking and spending generously on his pleasures.

One young Negro was a vivid illustration of these confusions as he related them to me in the presence of a large group of his peers. Now eighteen, he had dropped out of school long ago. He held a good job for some months but it was given to a white boy. Since then, for almost a year he had not worked nor had he tried seriously to find a job. When asked about plans for his future, he merely shrugged. (Later the worker explained that this boy got his income from shooting pool and gambling; at both he is expert.) The climax came when he talked about being questioned on the street late at night by the police. With great feeling, especially indignant at what he regarded as the injustice of it, he shouted, "I am eighteen! I am a man!" He later referred to his "mother-in-law" but there had been no wedding ceremony with the "wife." He was in a kind of no man's land of patches of adulthood.

The crucial variables in this rites of passage dilemma are sublower-class and minority status, with the roads to fuller adulthood largely blocked. Unless meaningful help is offered in the way of accessible opportunities and the ability to use them, the future looks dark for a large number of American youth. The streetworkers and many others are struggling all but heroically with this problem but available resources are pitifully inadequate.

## The Situational Approach

People have argued that by cutting down on temptations and stimuli, delinquency can be substantially decreased. Specific measures are curfews, eliminating the cruder forms of violence from the mass media, reducing the number of sexually stimulating publications available to youth, keeping down the resources for obtaining liquor, increasing recreational facilities, and any other steps which curtail the opportunities for delinquent acts. The enactment of most of these measures presents complications. The curfew, for example, is applied to all youth and cannot be limited to those who are delinquency-prone. Is it fair to the others? Controlling the amount of unfortunate stimulation in the mass media raises questions of censorship. In many instances there are laws which prohibit the sale of liquor to those under twenty-one, yet there is a high incidence of drinking by youth. It is extremely difficult to enforce the letter and intent of such laws.

In another dimension, it is probable that such measures would not affect significantly the more seriously delinquent. When values are distorted and supported by a subculture, when legitimate opportunities are meager, when psychopathology is strong, youngsters will find ways to be delinquent. Changing the situation or the environmental stimuli can have the effect of altering the triggers and patterns of their actions, but basic tensions in such young people are not apt to be relieved. If, for example, automobile manufacturers were to make it very difficult—as they should—to steal cars, that form of theft would probably decrease but the amount of stealing by true delinquents might not. Accompanying some of these measures, such as the curfew, may be a challenge to the delinquent to get around them, thereby perhaps adding laws for him to break.

For those who are borderline delinquents, it may well be that strong stimuli in the mass media or being out on the streets late at night could trigger off delinquent acts. Generally, however, the situational approach seems to be more superficial than the others. It may be needed when conflict is rampant or when it is clear that a cluster of incidents occur in an infectious area for obvious reasons, but we should have modest expectations for what it can accomplish.

## Multiple Causation

Delinquency is not a unitary diagnostic category. It is behavior which is in conflict with the law within a designated age range. Its origins are diverse not only from one youth to another but also within any one youngster. While it may be neater intellectually and seemingly easier to do research when commitment is made to one single theory of causation and one isolated method of intervention, the forces operating are so interwoven that a disservice is done to the complexities of delinquency. No matter what lever is used, it is essential to utilize all others which are relevant. Take one example, the opportunity blockage theory: the action program that follows will effect changes which encourage more education and which lead to the placement of the young people in suitable and satisfying jobs. As professionals work with the youngsters in this program, psychological processes are generated which involve psychodynamic theory. Aspects of the subculture will have to be tackled. And so it goes.

There is danger in the multiple causation position of intellectual laziness, of "it depends" kind of loose thinking. Theorists and practitioners need to practice rigorous diagnostic assessment which relates the facts in each situation to whatever theories enlighten and give meaning to them, so that appropriate action can be taken.

## The Need for New Theory

There has been a gratifying intensification of the questioning of old theories and the searching for new ones. This is healthy and encouraging. Out of this ferment may come some excellent ideas. But a note of caution is in order on the case for discarding old theories. We need to scrutinize the theory and the situation to which it was applied to try to determine whether the inadequacies, especially in terms of results, arose out of:

1) Defects in the theory itself.
2) Staff insufficient or incompetent to test it fairly. The delinquency field is shot full of examples of trying to do too much with too little. This is a most urgent consideration. Work with delinquency is slow, painstaking and massive. Relatively few programs have ever had sufficient resources to test fairly their theoretical bases.

3) Social changes such as a large influx of population containing many potential delinquents. New delinquents could be pumped into the area faster than a good program based on the best theory can deal with the old ones.

## Rationale for Streetwork

The rationale for streetwork with groups needs to be presented to round out the theoretical framework for this book, and to provide a base for one of its central recommendations for dealing with important aspects of delinquency. In the search for new methods we should not overlook an available one which has both actual and much more potential strength.

The more hostile, sublower-class youth groups do not fit readily into the more or less traditional building-centered youth service programs, such as are found in Y's, settlements, Boys Clubs and the like, nor into other organizations primarily suitable for conforming youngsters, such as the Scouts. It should be added that some of the group service agencies have recognized this fact and have creatively developed the reaching-out-on-the-streets type of approach. The distinction here is not so much between agencies as it is between kinds of programs.

The more aggressive youth groups either do not go to the in-the-building programs which are designed for a cross-section of the young people, or, if they go, their behavior creates tensions and frequently they are evicted. What may be otherwise reasonable rules about smoking, drinking, bad language, and fighting, for these hostile young people are challenges to battle and test. Furthermore, the better-behaved youngsters feel threatened by and resent (as often do their parents) the rougher ones. There may, and often does, come a time when the aggressive group is ready to abide by the requirements in the organization but much good work must precede this stage, and a sensitive diagnosis is essential to avoid prematurity and its ensuing eruptions.

It would be a deplorable oversimplification to reduce this cleavage between the hostile groups and agencies which cannot abide their behavior to mere aggression. Beneath the external defiance, a deep river flows. These groups and their members have usually experienced repeated rejection by many representatives of the com-

munity. Their sense of self-worth has been damaged. They feel that most of the respectable world is against them. They have models and precedents for their belligerence. Their emotional economy cannot take the chance of profit and loss from conforming; the fear of rejection is usually too great. Security is found in group aggression and in fulfilling their belief that the agency is against them, as have been, in their perceptions, the school, the police and others. Hence, the best defense is an attack.

They make the street corner, the alley, the playground or the poolroom their community center, just so that they can set their own rules and have demands on them limited to those which they can respect and handle. Many are highly undisciplined, able to exert relatively little control over their impulses. They crave excitement and are weak in the ability to anticipate the consequences of their behavior. These states are not permanent or irrevocable, but are usually the ones in which the worker finds them.

Out of these and other factors there was developed the idea of sending a worker to deal with these youngsters in their native habitat. In the early days, there was much concern about reaching them and diverse ideas about how to do it. This is no longer an issue. They can and they have been reached, with relatively few exceptions. Indeed, there are even examples of unserved groups acting dramatically anti-social to secure the attention and services of a worker. Unfortunately, it has not always been possible to provide one.

At earlier stages, it was assumed that establishing a good relationship and doing high-level group work with the gang and with individual members would produce the desired results. Now the thinking is more sophisticated and the general social situation facing these young people is more vividly understood. Important as are the dynamics of their personalities and their group, the worker's efforts are conditioned by the extent that he can tap resources to move them on the way to functioning as somewhat settled and productive adults. Relationships in the present for turbulent adolescents take on more constructive meaning as they pave the road through the rites of passage.

Yet the streetworker may be alone, or have only little company, in being close to the daily living of the youngsters, to their crises, to their sense of trust. He is part of their lives in a way that is

often unique. He can be a connecting link between them and services and opportunities. Whatever other programs are designed for alienated youth groups in our slums, the streetworker should be central, the point of contact.

## Conditions

There would be little profit in building good theory and methods if we did not take full account of socio-economic conditions. Here we meet a combination of disturbing forces which could be called diabolical if they were deliberately planned. Probably all times in history pound some people, but sublower-class youth are special victims now. Thunderbolts are not being hurled at them, but barriers have been built which have an impact as potent as the Berlin Wall. Nobody particularly meant to build them, but there they are, not physical edifices but just as real.

The much-discussed growth of automation is one of their prime building blocks. Jobs for the unskilled have not been increasing. More and more of the available jobs require skills, education, and sophistication in human relations which are out of the world of the youth who are the subject of this book. They know about this development and painfully face the choice between meeting its requirements and maintaining their way of life. Feelings are mixed and confused, with some deciding one way and some choosing another. But sadly, their decisions are just single little straws in powerful winds.

To compound the situation, there are so many of these young people. When they were innocently born, they did not know that they were contributing to a population explosion, but an explosion it is.

To provide some illustrative facts, the *increase* in the Negro population of Detroit is lined up as follows: [6]

Under 15 years of age:

| | |
|---|---|
| 1940–1950 | 113% |
| 1950–1960 | 131% |
| 1960–1970 | 51% |

[6] Thomas F. Hoult and Albert J. Mayer, *The Population Revolution in Detroit* (Detroit: Institute for Regional and Urban Studies, Wayne State University, 1963), p. 3.

15 to 24 years of age:

| | |
|---|---|
| 1940–1950 | 87% |
| 1950–1960 | 25% |
| 1960–1970 | 74% |

These increases are staggering and, while the details differ in other large cities, the trends are similar.

Extending the scope of the data, Ewan Clague predicts that in the 1960-1970 decade, *twenty-six million* young people will have entered the labor market.[7] In the same article he provides figures to show that the high percentages of Negroes are concentrated in the unskilled or less-skilled occupations. He also supports factually the continuing status quo in the number of unskilled jobs, yet the number of unskilled job seekers is increasing enormously. The number of skilled jobs is growing.

In the face of a shrinking market for the unskilled and the wrong-skilled, young people are entering it each year at an alarming rate, and many of them are from the sublower class, without much to offer. Unions are fighting what seems to be a losing battle against automation and some seem to have little patience with pleas for undisciplined youth. Heads of families, with justification, get priority. But where can these young people go economically? What strength can appeals for law-abiding behavior have in the face of a powerful disinheritance, which looks permanent? The rewards of virtue are not at all clear.

The big appeal made to such youth is the cash value of an education. Figures are cited to show how much more is earned by high school graduates, still more by college graduates. The future for school dropouts is pictured as indeed dreary. Yet we have not found ways for many of these youth to function satisfactorily in school. Some gratifying progress is being made in education for them, but far too little and too late. In talking with them, the psychological distance of many from school emerged clearly. Some bridged it with help; others did not.

Many raised the realistic question about whether high school graduation would assure them of a good job, citing examples to the

---

[7] Ewan Clague, Commissioner of Labor Statistics, U.S. Department of Labor, "Demographic Trends and Their Significance," *The Changing American Population,* 1962, p. 15 (a report of the Ardon House Conference).

contrary. The sense they gave of what it would take out of them to achieve a high school diploma was saddening, and this herculean effort might be in vain. Not one of them regarded education as desirable in itself. All saw its value as utilitarian in terms of jobs, a state of affairs far from absent in the middle class. Yet the utilitarian end may be a mirage. There is the further complication that jobs which become available to them may be dull, poor-paying and dead-end. Why beat one's brains out in school to learn how to wash cars or sweep floors?

The stress is increased by unrealistic expectations on the part of many of these young people. While the family income is apt to come from public welfare or from one—sometimes two—parents in an unskilled and low-paid job, the abundance around them, legitimate and illegitimate, has affected their expectations. As one boy put it: "Why should I break my back for $46 a week?" The boy didn't seem to realize that his "back" was all he had to offer. On another occasion, when the writer asked a group about their occupational aspirations, they mentioned architecture, electrical engineering and other fields which require a high level of education. Only one wanted auto mechanics. It was suggested that most of them did not want to get their hands dirty. There was practically a roar of commitment to this clean thesis. How neat the fit will be between their teenage aspirations and life as it will be lived gives one sharp pause.

And there is still more disruption, namely vast population movement. Charles E. Silberman [8] indicates that most of the large shift of Negro population from the South to the North has been to the twelve largest metropolitan areas; all nine cities visited by the author in the preparation of this book are included in his list.

To cite the Detroit study again,[9] it indicates a major trend toward moving out of the city by those able to do so, leaving a population who face severe economic, educational and housing restrictions. The writers of the study estimate that by 1970 a very large percentage of the people living in Detroit will be young Negroes and older whites. The implications of these trends for the futures of our large cities are tremendous, but they are beyond the scope of this book and the competence of its author.

---

[8] Charles E. Silberman, "The City and the Negro," *Fortune*, March, 1962.
[9] Hoult & Mayer, *op. cit.*, p. 8.

The impact of population movement on sublower-class youth and their families is diverse and deep. Many of them come from rural or other areas in which they did not learn to deal with the congestion and complexities of the urbanized ghetto. Often their education has been most inadequate. Latin-Americans face an additional language problem. There have been instances of teenagers who, having not gone beyond the lower grades in their previous setting, are not at all equipped to meet the requirements of the grade which corresponds to their age in the big city.

Additionally these great population changes in our cities often mean that neighborhood people have not had the time—and frequently not the skills—to form and maintain organizations and to develop generally a social structure and mores which encourage and support constructive values and behavior in young people. Acute examples of this condition are large housing developments. Much good work has been done in some of them, but in many, the destructive standards create fertile opportunities for the more violent and aggressive to set the tone. The courage to deal firmly with disturbing behavior tends to grow only as the residents feel the support of their neighbors and the strength that comes with organization. Skilled professionals are usually needed to stimulate such joint efforts.

A final element in this listing of obstacles is the actuality of belonging to a minority group, whether on a racial, ethnic or class basis, with all its related deprivations. It was a troubling experience to find a tendency on the part of many of the youngsters to deny that being in a minority was a problem and to be reluctant to discuss the subject. It may be a defense mechanism to wipe out psychologically a painful reality. Yet, when we were discussing such specifics as jobs, the quality of the neighborhood, education and relations with the police, they would frequently refer to instances of prejudice. Some workers expressed concern about the tendency on the part of the youngsters to deny that prejudice was a problem to them and to be reluctant to talk about it, even with a worker of the same background.

This was the situation during the winter and spring of 1963. Now (summer, 1963) Negro protests and demonstrations have acquired great momentum, with a new and dramatic impact on the country. It would be interesting to go back to the same cities, workers and

youngsters to ascertain what changes have occurred. One hopes that the Negro youth in the more hostile groups are deriving from this national development a new sense of dignity. There is the danger that they will use the new situation primarily to meet their own emotional needs, especially those involving aggression and power. This is occurring in an institution for delinquents where some Negro boys are making life difficult for all. The irony is that they are distorting the ideals and the spirit of non-violence of much of the Negro leadership, an understandable phenomenon.

Another concern deals with what is happening during the ferment within non-Negro minority groups, such as Puerto Ricans, Mexican-Americans, Indians and others. Will their young people view this struggle as one which will benefit all minorities or only as something especially for Negroes?

With the rising tide of protest, the mood of resignation by Negroes and others to deprivation is diminishing. They are now demanding what should not have been necessary to ask for. Just what the sublower-class youth will do with this new mood remains to be seen, but they certainly will be affected by it. The challenge to them is in what more thoughtful Negro leaders are urging, i.e., along with the opening up of opportunities by whites, Negroes should prepare responsibly to take advantage of their new opportunities. The temptation for aggressive young people will be to fight rather than to equip themselves. They need help in making the transition toward more planned and responsible behavior.

With various theories and socio-economic conditions before us, we are now ready to look at the young people themselves.

## CHAPTER TWO

HOW DIFFICULT BEHAVIOR is presented depends very much on the feelings of the presentor, on how he defines the situation. We tend to think of delinquent and generally anti-social behavior as objectively defined by law and moral standards, but how officials and other people view the situation is a significant component of the

# groups, behavior, problems and Values

definition. As an illustration, there is an "adolescent moratorium" notion, confined mainly to middle-class youth, which accepts, admits and forgives their flings. There is also the unfortunate notion that when sublower-class youth bang up each other, the rest of us can shrug resignedly; when they rob or injure middle-class people, they are "hoodlums."

Having had many times the experience of being with what seemed to be extremely hostile and forbidding youngsters who later, with a trusting relationship established, turned out to be interesting, appealing, and sometimes charming and talented human beings, the writer is suspicious of static categories which label and even condemn people. Yet there is an important factual side to behavior. What follows is an attempt to present it with due regard for the dangers of rigid and sweeping generalizations.

**Trends in Groupings**

A. Boys

The large, highly structured gang has diminished, but not disappeared. In New York, Chicago, Philadelphia and a few other

cities there were reported to be some examples of what is called the
vertical gang, i.e., with subunits built on age levels, sometimes with
female auxiliaries. But predominant in all of the nine cities were
the smaller groups, often called "clusters," frequently without obvious symbols such as jackets. There were examples of groups
making their identity highly public by writing the group name on
walls and in other ways letting the community know about their
existence. This, however, was not the predominant trend. In Syracuse, New York,[1] no highly organized gangs were found, and the
work of the Huntington-Gifford Project was done with clusters
whose memberships were not altogether stable.

Why adolescent boys who enjoy the excitement and power of
being part of a large and clearly identified group should settle for
smaller and, in a sense, quieter groups, is an intriguing and important question. Professionals close to the situation suggested plausi-
ble explanations. The police have developed an elaborate approach
to gangs, with a file in some instances which includes the name of
the gang as a whole and of its known members, as well as their
nicknames, addresses, and other information. In Detroit, it is the
practice of the Gang Detail of the Youth Bureau to meet with vulnerable young people and their parents to discuss what the law
requires and related issues. Active efforts are made to break up
larger and more destructive gangs. The boys seem to be aware of
these activities and adopt quieter and less visible ways of expressing
their impulses.

A second factor in the trend toward smaller and less formal
groups is the work of the agencies which serve them. Rather consistently, their focus is on one age level, and smaller and more
reachable groups. When the vertical group exists, the aim is to
separate the subunits. It is usually desirable and even necessary for
the worker to give some attention to older subunits, but the greatest effort is devoted to one age range.

A third element in this development is the reaction of parents
and others in the neighborhood to large and dramatic incidents. In
Hunter's Point in San Francisco, for example, hostility developed
between Negro and Samoan boys, and a battle was scheduled. The

---

[1] Norman R. Roth, *Reaching the Hard-to-Reach, A Report of the Huntington-Gifford Project on Hard to Reach Youth,* (Huntington Family Centers,
[Syracuse, New York, 1961]), p. 35, p. 90.

Samoans came armed with their machetes and the consequences could well have been serious. Fortunately, the police were informed and the battle was prevented. Parents were upset, the administrators of the housing development threatened to put out the families of the warriors, and there were other reactions. The impact was strong enough to discourage further large-scale fighting.

There is the danger of finding too much comfort and reassurance in the trend toward smaller and less visible groups of antisocial youngsters. To a degree, they have learned how to play the game, and have become more sophisticated. The argument has been used that streetwork is not needed because gang rumbles have decreased, as though the rumbles were the only problem. There are many others just as serious, and changes in styles of association do not necessarily solve problems and launch the youngsters successfully on the way to healthy adulthood.

The strong negative reactions to the idea of large and well-organized gangs can lead us to overlook the functions which a group can serve for the sublower class youngster. It may be the only area in which he finds satisfactions and identity. All too often his family is not a source of pride. When, as is frequently true, he is of a minority background, this aspect of his identity does not tend to sustain and build him. Difficult experiences with middle-class institutions and people frequently alienate him. Added to all of this are the powerful forces in all adolescents which turn them toward their peers, regardless of their social class. For the alienated youngster, the group is often the real world, the frame of reference.

Many instances were reported of two categories in relation to the group: core members and peripheral ones. Much needs yet to be discovered about the characteristics of each. One hypothesis is that the boys in the families of a lowest-class neighborhood who are upwardly mobile are apt to be the core and leadership members of such groups. In some cases, the point was made that the gesture of joining the group may be motivated more by the protection it offers against other groups than by any positive appeal. However, in one Chicago area it was found that about half the boys were not in gangs.

Interesting classifications have been developed for these groups. Cloward and Ohlin [2] suggest three types: conflict, criminal and re-

[2] Cloward & Ohlin, *op. cit.*

treatist. They are meant as ideal types not found in a pure state. Those interviewed in this study largely support the existence of a mixture of two or of all three in many instances. The conflict type, which seems to be the great bulk of those served by the agencies, has reduced its fighting as a whole group; it practically always includes individuals who have engaged in other kinds of delinquent activity. The retreatist pattern, as far as the serious use of drugs by adolescents is concerned, is relatively unusual and limited to certain cities to be discussed below. There is a great deal of group drinking but it does not seem to have the retreatist quality as described by Cloward and Ohlin.

A refinement of the Cloward and Ohlin typology is presented by Spergel.[3] He suggests the categories of racket, conflict and theft, adding as a fourth, the drug group, and relates each to the socio-economic backgrounds of the members, with special emphasis on the opportunities available, legitimate and illegitimate, to them. The racket group is integrated with a criminal way of life in the neighborhood. In relation to potentials for change, Spergel thinks that the racket group is very difficult because its mores derive so much neighborhood support, the conflict group can be helped only through the massive opening of legitimate opportunities, and the drug addicts are extremely difficult to change, but the theft category lends itself best to a social work approach and is the most prevalent kind of anti-social group. He points out that his framework has a limited base in data. His position helps to clarify some of the patterns of these groups in relation to their families and neighborhoods, but again caution should be used about firm generalizations applied to all large cities.

A different category pattern was developed out of the practice of the Group Guidance Section of the Los Angeles County Probation Department. The "area" or "neighborhood" gang develops where the population has been relatively stable and a gang tradition has existed, sometimes for generations. Such gangs tend to be reinforced by neighborhood attitudes and are highly cohesive. Although the core active members may not be numerous, the total number is usually large, often with subgroups according to age levels. Attempts to break up such gangs are apt to fail and may drive

---

[3] Irving Spergel, "An Exploratory Research in Delinquent Subcultures," *Social Service Review,* XXXV, No. 1, (March, 1961).

the group underground. The more hopeful approach is to accept the gang as a reality and try to redirect its energies.

The "spontaneous" gang, on the other hand, does not have a tradition to nourish and stimulate it. Specific interests draw the members together, and when they reach the end of the teen years, the group dissolves naturally without passing along the torch to a younger edition. Under certain conditions, the spontaneous group may develop into an area gang. This seems to be a classification useful in helping to understand antisocial groups.

There are other frameworks for classifying these groups, but it is well to move on and consider their composition, again drawing on the Los Angeles Group Guidance Section. Based on a study (1961-62) of 497 boys who were members of gangs, the distribution of the boys was reported as follows:

| | | |
|---|---|---|
| Total chronically gang-oriented | 70 or | 14% |
| Total situationally gang-oriented | 311 or | 62.8% |
| Total non-delinquent | 116 or | 23.2% |
| Total | 497 | 100% |

The non-delinquent figure was based on the absence of their names from police, probation and parole records. The other two categories were influenced some by such records, but the primary determinants were the knowledge and judgment of the workers (probation officers) dealing with the groups.

I do not know how rigorous a process was followed in developing these figures, nor how they would compare with a similar tabulation in other cities. Even, however, if one were to assume that they are only approximate, they are interesting and significant, especially for the distinctions they make.[4] What is called the "chronically gang-oriented" boy, sometimes referred to as the "gang psycho" by the same Group Guidance Section, and as the "gang war butch" by a worker in the Crime Prevention Association of Philadelphia, often has a history of psychopathology in his own and his family's background. Typically he is a school dropout with little if any satisfactory work history. His family relationships are

---

[4] What follows is suggested but not so defined by the Los Angeles Group Guidance Section. The writer may have taken liberties with their ideas, but the patterns described have much significance for what was found in the cities visited.

usually frustrating. In short, the gang is the only area in which he finds satisfaction and can function. It tends to be the whole of life to him and he fights fiercely against attempts to dissolve the group or to change its character. The Los Angeles figure of 14% in this category seems high and it may be that the boundaries of their definition went beyond those just described. Whatever the figures may be, the concept of the gang psycho identifies a serious problem prevalent in all of the cities visited, and one which has persistently resisted existing methods of solving it.

The "situationally gang-oriented" category presents quite a different constellation. Here the pathology is in the neighborhood more than in the individual boy. A good case could be presented for the healthy aspects of gang participation by boys in such neighborhoods. The alternative might be even more destructive for the boys and for the community. This point has vast implications for intervention and it is rooted in the subculture and opportunity theories of delinquency. According to the Los Angeles figures, these are the bulk of the gang members, 62.8%, and presumably they have delinquent records.

The third category, the "non-delinquent," suggests that there are unusual strengths in these youngsters, with perhaps the qualification that they have managed not to get caught. The pressures upon them are apparently great enough to stimulate them to join active gangs, yet they do not participate in the delinquent acts to the extent of getting caught in them. The figure of 23.2% in this category is encouraging and we need to know much more about them. They present a leverage for change in gangs.

In addition to the primary group characteristics which have been considered, there are some broader and vaguer loyalties which are difficult to assess, but they keep coming up and should not be neglected. In Chicago some workers made quite a distinction between the "Ivy Leaguers" and the "Gowsers" (spelling uncertain). The youngsters seemed to know what Ivy League means and they dress accordingly. The Gowsers have rejected this middle-class concept. In Philadelphia there was the notion of the Tenderloin. Apparently this was a status to be achieved by the toughest, most powerful, and greatly feared. A group which won this appellation reached gang heaven. There were also the Yaks, who wore fancy clothes and were upwardly mobile. In San Francisco there were

(1) the Bloods, flashily dressed Negroes, (2) the Barts, ethnic group, Caucasians wearing their hair in ducktail style with a curl on the forehead, bedecked in rough, tough-looking clothes, and (3) the White Shoes, lower middle-class Caucasians, upwardly mobile, with crew-cut hair and white buck shoes. In Los Angeles there was the difference between the Surfers, Anglos wearing tight jeans, and the Hodads, Mexican-Americans. Other cities' groups probably adopt these larger identities through which teenagers seek selfhood. A rich teenage folklore is evidenced here, and quite a study could be made of its variety and significance.

The most meaningful object for identity seems to be geographic. It may be "turf," consisting of a block as in some sections of New York, or a whole district, town, or housing project. The basic quality of this association was illustrated in a "truce-meeting" between representatives of two warring gangs. The boys repeatedly referred to outsiders coming into "our town." A staff member challenged them by saying that they didn't own it; there was a government and privately owned property. The reaction was a mixture of puzzlement and uneasy tolerance. All they could say was, "You know, man, this is our town." Some values go so deep that the only way to discuss them is to reiterate them. In this respect these boys are not too different from the rest of us. We all seem to be devoted to real estate, regardless of whether we own it, and much blood has been spilled over the centuries in this cause.

## B. Girls

Here too the range of behavior is such that every facet of it could be illustrated, from the most lurid and violent to the staid and respectable. Generally it seems true that girls have not developed well-organized and cohesive anti-social groups to anything like the extent that boys have. There have been some such girls' groups, at times the auxiliaries of boys' gangs, but this has been decreasing.

It should be stated that girls have received only a fraction of the amount of attention given to boys, and therefore our knowledge of girls' groups is substantially less. There is the curious folklore notion that girls need less attention and service, and that if the boys are straightened out, the girls will fall in line, an assumption that seems to have little justification.

Many instances were reported of girls instigating fights between boys' groups. The truce-meeting in Los Angeles cited above was a juicy illustration. Representatives of the battling groups kept referring to what Mary (fictitious name) told each about the other. At several points, there was a shocked, "She said that!" Mary had done quite a job and apparently enjoyed being fought about. The boys seemed to be catching on to her machinations. This was one pattern.

On the other hand there were illustrations of efforts by girls to promote peace and decency. There were examples of girls carrying weapons for the boys, not always voluntarily, but the helpful influences of femininity were also present. It is certainly true that the sublower-class female faces an arduous and even bleak existence. She tends to feel very much exploited.

The relationship of the girls' groups to the boys' ran the gamut from being clearly auxiliaries, even having the same names as the boys' groups with "ettes" added to them, to no stable relationship with any one boys' group, with freedom of movement for the girls individually or collectively from one set of boys to another. The latter state lends itself to conflict among boys in competing for girls.

There was some fighting reported among the girls but with much less frequency than among boys. A few instances were related, of rather recent origin, of violent aggression, even viciousness, among girls' groups.

### Leadership

It is generally agreed that leadership is crucial for the life of a group as well as for the potential success of work with it. Thinking in the field of group dynamics emphasizes the close relationship between the characteristics of leadership and the mores, values and aspirations of the group. It is not surprising, then, to find that many leaders of hostile groups embody abilities prized by their members. Two particular qualities stand out: physical prowess, especially in fighting, and a quick and often biting tongue, accompanied by the ability to think fast and to come up with ideas or wisecracks pleasing to the others. An interesting instance was related of a boy obviously smaller and weaker than the others, yet

with a facility for talking them into or out of anything. He was clearly the leader.

There may be examples in which the same boy is the leader in all situations, but many instances to the contrary were cited. For a fight, it would be the toughest, or the wiliest for planning strategy. For settling conflicts among the members or for making plans for non-fighting activities, it is likely to be the coolest head, and not necessarily the most aggressive.

A dramatic picture of gang leadership is presented by Yablonsky,[5] who studied many gangs in the Upper West Side of Manhattan. Before dealing with his ideas of leadership, it is essential to look at his typology of gangs:

1) Those which are primarily delinquent with a number of stable members and some cohesiveness and continuity. They may be relatively small.

2) The "social" gang, which is tough in its behavior and yet finds acceptable outlets for its energies, such as dances and athletics.

3) The "violent" gang, comprised largely of "sociopaths" with volatile emotions, seeking prestige through violence, and searching for "kicks" regardless of how much they hurt people in obtaining them. The book cites many illustrations of indulgence in violence without much sense of remorse or guilt. The great value is violence. The famous killing of Michael Farmer, the New York boy crippled by polio, is a prime illustration used by Yablonsky. The victim was not even a member of the gang against which his killers wanted to retaliate.

Keeping in mind that his book is largely concerned with the violent gang, and that Yablonsky claims that they are numerous, he presents the leaders of such groups as sociopaths whose lives have been full of frustration, who try to become significant human beings through building and manipulating the power and violence of the gang. This is the stuff of their fantasies and their behavior, a forbidding picture indeed.

An implication for intervention drawn by Yablonsky is that these leaders should not be reinforced or dignified in any way; they should be undermined and their groups dissipated. If Yablonsky

---

[5] Lewis Yablonsky, *The Violent Gang* (New York: The Macmillan Co., 1962).

is right about leadership, his recommendations follow logically and
the practices of various agencies should be changed. Especially to
be eliminated is the truce meeting between representatives of battling gangs. In Yablonsky's context, this would place sociopaths in
positions of prestige and power, which they would use destructively.

Yablonsky in his book presents three kinds of gangs, and his
conclusions about leadership would seem to apply only to the violent category. There is an obligation to find out whether this type
predominates in whatever area is under consideration.

Now let's turn to what was generally reported in the nine cities
visited about psychopathic leadership. There were occasional instances cited of the gang psycho rising to a position of leadership,
but they were exceptions and special circumstances were apt to
account for such occurrences. Many groups were reported as including some pathological individuals but they tended to lead only
when their reckless aggression met contagious conditions. If something had happened such as an attack by rivals, which stirred the
emotions of the group, the violently aggressive boy might supply
the trigger. Occasionally, with the sicker kind of group, he could
win a more stable position of leadership. Far more frequently he
was described as the instigator, the fomenter, rather than the leader.
This was said in New York as well as elsewhere.

These points about leadership have been elaborated because of
their significance for community programs. If the great majority
of the leaders are psychologically sick, the sound approach would
be to get them out of the community and into settings where psychiatric treatment would be given to them, probably not by choice.
If, on the other hand, many of these leaders are relatively healthy
individuals, as I believe they are, responding to difficult social situations, the difficulty is not the same and the programs should be
different. How we perceive the problems has great bearing on what
we do about them, and leaders are keys by which significant doors
can be unlocked.

## Kinds of Delinquent Behavior

Frequently mentioned were car thefts, other types of stealing,
shakedowns of younger children, drinking, making and using weapons (several agencies had quite a collection of vicious-looking ones

taken away from the youngsters), illicit sexual behavior and fight-ing. Over and over again it was said that these activities were rarely engaged in by the group as a whole, but rather were the acts of one, two, three or four. If the group is known as such in the neighborhood, it tended to be tarred as a whole with the brush of the delinquency of some of its members. There is the problem of group acceptance of the deviant behavior of some or most mem-bers, but there is the danger in this kind of stereotyping that the better-behaved youngsters will be stimulated to emulate the others. Youth can be unfortunately obliging with this sort of expectation of them.

The story was told in Chicago of a streetworker who had done the same work in New York. As he was getting acquainted with the boys in a Chicago neighborhood, he asked them where their turf was. The term and the idea were not familiar to them, and they responded with a blank, "Huh?" Whereupon the worker in-structed them in the meaning of turf. They thought this a great idea, and soon that section of Chicago was full of turfs.

Often, in less obvious ways, the assumptions and expectations of adults have their impact. Terms like "a gang of hoodlums" are a challenge to live up to the reputation or to give up associations with peers which frequently have great meaning. We easily fall into the trap of regarding the troublesome behavior as congealed and unitary, whereas behind it there are usually conflicts, admixtures of desires to behave differently and some individuals who need only a little help to move in other directions. There are groups in which the delinquent tendencies are so strong that the pressures on the members to conform to the group's mores are all but ir-resistible. There are many, however, in which there is an uneasy and volatile mixture, and an unfortunate occurrence can easily com-mit all to delinquency. It is the job of responsible adults to sup-port the strengths in the whole group and in each of its members, avoiding the dangers of stereotyping.

### Rumbles and Other Kinds of Fighting

While peace has not broken out in our slums, there has been a remarkable decrease in rumbles. This term can be defined as a

large, organized and planned fight between two gangs, at times assisted by allies, in which some of the paraphernalia of war ("war councilors," weapons, etc.) are apt to be present. "West Side Story" presents an example of this on a relatively small scale. In some cases in the past the numbers of protagonists were larger, although one must discount the tendencies of both warriors and the adults they shock to exaggerate the size and scope of the battle. But even in some cities, especially Chicago, where such events had reached alarming proportions, the consistent reports from those in the know were that rumbles had dramatically decreased. Why?

In addition to factors cited earlier, there is often an eye on the whole area which watches for trouble spots in which streetwork agencies operate. For example, a supervisor in the Chicago Youth Centers was driving the writer to a hotel late in the evening. He stopped to watch a collection of boys, possibly drunk, arguing heatedly. He shouted, "Cool it, man, I don't want to see you get into trouble." They glared at him and muttered what seemed to be epithets, but they did move on and probably an incident was averted. In the Youth Development Project of the Chicago Boys Clubs, the practice was for one of the administrative or supervisory personnel to tour the area in his car every evening of the week.

In still another agency, the problem was that the geographic location of schools was such as to make it necessary for Negroes to go through white neighborhoods and vice versa. After-school fights were serious. At the beginning of an interview with the staff members of the United Neighbors Association in Philadelphia, they prepared the writer for an interruption when schools let out. Sure enough, at the precise time, we all went to the prepared spots. We saw teachers watching the youngsters leave school, but their responsibilities seemed to end on that block. This was a quiet day. The only incident was the breaking of a bottle on the sidewalk. As the executive predicted, an irate housewife (white) appeared. He got out of the car to tell her that white boys had done it. So explosive can these situations be that his little act may have prevented rumors and subsequent mayhem.

On a deeper level, whatever success the streetworkers and others have achieved in helping the youngsters to find legitimate

ways to live and express themselves, has channeled their interests and energies away from rumbles and other kinds of fighting. There were numerous examples, in the face of great difficulties, of success in this direction.

While rumbles on a large scale have decreased, there is still much fighting by members of these alienated youth groups. A form of it, called "snagging" or "Japping," was said to be fairly common in New York by an executive of the New York City Youth Board, and it was mentioned in some but not all of the nine cities. A lookout watches the regular movements of one or two members of an antagonistic group. When it is established that a suitable place will be passed at a predictable time by the victim(s), about six of the aggressors go home, wash and shave, put on their good suits, and then saunter casually toward that spot. They are careful to go in pairs and not to show in any way by their behavior what is afoot. When the victims(s) comes along, they give him or them a bad beating, and then wend their externally casual way home to change clothes. Elsewhere, the ritual was different in that they would not risk their one good suit in a fight. The planning was such as to assure the quick success of the enterprise. In either instance, the victim need not be a previous aggressor, just associated with the rival group.

Dances and house parties, without responsible adults present, are fertile breeding occasions for fights. Drinking is apt to occur and, as one boy said, "There is always a bad apple" (always someone else) who starts something. The losers try, often successfully, to get their friends to retaliate.

Still another form of fighting is called the "fair one" in which a representative of each group fights without weapons or assistance from his friends. A high percentage of fair ones which are talked about do not actually occur. The fight calls for a level of self-discipline which is difficult for these boys. It also puts the two fighters in a very tense position. The prospective loser is in too emotionally charged and semi-public a spot, and it is understandable that many times the fight does not actually take place. Workers discourage fair ones.

There is a significant question about those involved in fights, i.e., between what categories of people is this aggression expressed

overtly? A mimeographed report [6] from the Group Guidance Section in Los Angeles, as of 1960, provides the following distribution:

12% of the gang incidents were assaults against adults; 88% against other juveniles.

About 20% were against individuals who were not members of gangs; 80% against gang members.

A deadly weapon was involved in 54% of the instances.

An ethnic (race and nationality) component was present in 18% of the cases.

The report suggests that there are probably many incidents which are not reported, but that the more serious ones do tend to come to official attention.

Another set of figures [7] deals with gang incidents according to race and ethnic background for the years 1960-62. Some highlights merit attention. For 1962, in descending frequency, these incidents were as follows:

| | |
|---|---|
| Negroes against Negroes | 220 |
| Negroes against Caucasians | 147 |
| Caucasians against Caucasians | 134 |
| Mexican-Americans against Mexican-Americans | 108 |
| Caucasians against Mexican-Americans | 78 |
| Mexican-Americans against Negroes | 42 |

If these figures are regrouped, we find 462, or 63% of the incidents involve groups of the same background as against 267, or 37% of the incidents involving groups of different backgrounds. Part of the explanation of incidents within the same racial or ethnic background would seem to be the ghetto arrangement of the population, i.e., there are more opportunities for conflict with youngsters living nearby and with whom there is more frequent contact. Yet many of these groups are mobile, especially in Los Angeles. The truce-meeting referred to above was between two Mexican-American groups living about forty miles apart.

---

[6] Al Collier, Senior Deputy Probation Officer, Group Guidance Section, Los Angeles Probation Department, "Gang Information System—Analysis and Interpretation," undated.

[7] Given to me by John A. Buggs, Executive Secretary of the Commission on Human Relations, County of Los Angeles, and compiled by the Los Angeles Police Department.

## Dress

Reference was made to the great preoccupation with having just the right kind of expensive suit. In other instances the pattern was to stress the hat and the shoes, with little concern for what was in between. Many devote great care to the hair, even to having it "processed" by a professional so that it would be just right. Fights were avoided for a time to preserve the hairdo. A rag was frequently worn around the hair. There were instances of earrings and other jewelry.

One can speculate on the significance to the boys of what looks to average middle-class eyes like bizarre dress. One possibility is that it has great identity meaning. It is clearly and visibly rebellious against the standards of dress of the larger community. Perhaps, similar to uniforms worn by members of more respectable organizations, it tells the world who and what they are. It also creates problems in schools and in getting jobs, where middle-class standards operate. It has the general quality of adolescent peer conformity.

There is also the feminine aspect of some elements of dress among these boys. One speculation is that since many of them come from matriarchal families, they do not have satisfactory male figures with whom to identify. This is compounded by what seems to be the greater availability of jobs for the minority female than for the male. Across the country workers expressed concern about the adequacy of the male identification of their boys; the extremes of male toughness and feminine attributes.

## Larger Movements

In some respects these groups of sublower-class young people would seem to be ripe for protest movements. But the workers reported that relatively few had joined the Black Muslims, the explanation being that this organization had little to offer which would meet their concrete needs, such as jobs. There were instances of work with the NAACP, but they seemed to involve the less hostile young people. In Boston a small number of white gang boys were picked up by the American Nazi Party.

It should be repeated that the interviews supplying this infor-

mation were held before the demonstrations and other protests reached their peak and they may have since made an impact. It is hoped that these adolescents will not succumb to the hate groups, which is a dangerous possibility. On the other hand, their participation in more rational protest movements, hopefully with professional help, could be healthy all around. The tide of racial and ethnic loyalties is rising around the world, with great potential both beneficial and destructive.

### Special Problems

Certain problems were mentioned in all of the cities visited, and they call for separate consideration.

### A. Drugs

There was widespread reference to "experimentation" with glue-sniffing, pep pills and other of the milder drugs. As one worker put it, these drugs give "a cheap drunk." Apparently not too many of the youngsters became addicts but the problem troubled the workers and they were puzzled about how to deal with it. The drugs used were usually easy to obtain and the excitement they produced had great appeal to some of the teenagers. Some stole prescription pads and learned how to imitate the doctors' writing. The attitudes toward their use varied from being generally accepted as a part of the group mores, to being rejected as a weakness not to be tolerated.

The use of the more serious drugs seemed to be confined to certain cities, with New York apparently having the worst problem, but with some groups of addicts in Chicago. Boston, Philadelphia and some other cities seem to have been very successful in keeping the more serious drugs out of the hands and skins of teenage groups.

Workers suggested that the addicts tended to come from families with the most acute problems and that their feeling about a constructive future for themselves was often hopeless. In New York it was commented that when these youngsters graduate from "bopping" (this activity is not thought to be appropriate by practically anybody after the teen years), and a healthy next step, such as a job or further education, is not realistically available, the resort is

often to drugs. The telling point was made that drug addiction, although it may be less blatant in disturbing the community, can do more damage to the young people than fighting. Furthermore, the costs of the drugs are so great as to make some form of criminal activity essential to raise the money. There was also the impression that real addiction occurs more frequently near the end of the teen years and older, although the writer was shown a group of addicts on the lower East Side of New York in the area of the Mobilization for Youth, who looked to be fifteen and sixteen years old. There was also the suggestion that some addicts drop the habit when they are in their thirties, but the evidence for this was not solid.

The volume of work with drug addict groups was much less than that with those indulging in other kinds of deviance. Yet there were some encouraging examples. A publication [8] by the New York City Youth Board describes the painstaking detail and careful thought devoted to a group of adolescent addicts over a period of three years. The results with the majority of the members were encouraging. As might be expected, there were some failures, and they were frankly reported. Also, periods of progress were interlarded with regression, and the worker needed endless patience, skill and, as the publication emphasizes, optimism. It claims that the acceptance of the "once a junkie, always a junkie" position would be fatal to this work.

Similar instances of a reasonable degree of success were reported elsewhere in New York and in Chicago. But the number of such group workers was small and our knowledge of the nature and extent of the problems of addiction groups and how to work with them is much more limited than it is for other deviant groups. It is an important area for research and experimentation, and for thorough cooperation by all agencies drawing on knowledge from all relevant disciplines. The fact that some cities have managed to hold this problem down to negligible proportions with vigorous action by police and other authorities against those who make drugs available to teenagers contains a potent lesson.

---

[8] *Reaching the Teen Age Addict: A Study of Street Club Work with a Group of Adolescent Users* (New York City Youth Board [undated]). Pages 46-48 offer good suggestions for methods and principles for this work.

## B. Drinking

Drinking, in many cases heavily enough to get quite drunk and to be arrested for it, was reported in all of the cities visited. It was relatively easy for the youth to obtain beer, wine and whiskey. A common method was to give an adult the money to buy it for them, rewarding him with money or a drink. By pooling their funds, enough would be available so that the group could have quite a party. "Under the influence," they frequently became involved in fights and other escapades.

The workers consistently made clear to the groups their disapproval of drinking by teenagers and the dangers for them and others which stem from it. A serious obstacle was the extent to which excessive drinking by adults was clearly visible to the young people and the fact that many adults even encouraged the teenagers to drink. Certainly a lot of drinking is seen and read about in the mass media.

The streetworkers and others were discouraged about the results of their efforts to decrease drinking among the adolescents. They tried various appeals. One worker used the approach of asking how they would feel if their little sisters were playing on a street where a drunken boy was driving. Another slant was to say that drinking in moderation by adults is all right, but is bad for teenagers. If they must drink, they should do it maturely, with moderation, and in private.

Excessive drinking was among the most difficult problems encountered among the alienated youth groups and it is clear that the methods available for dealing with it are not sufficiently effective. Perhaps more emphasis could be put on a total neighborhood approach. Drinking, like drug addiction, is a problem in which the frontiers of our knowledge need to be pushed back through experimentation and research.

## C. Sex and Unmarried Mothers

Sex inhibitions were not strong among the teenagers under discussion, a problem not limited to the lower class. As one worker put it, "My boys have no sex problems" meaning that they expressed the urge freely. There was some mention of a decrease in promiscuity, with a degree of faithfulness between a couple as long

as the pairing off lasted. The "gang bang" or "line-up," in which a group of boys had successive intercourse with one girl whether force was used or not, seemed to be a rare occurrence. Some youngsters were resorting to a kind of informal trial marriage, with a degree of constancy, even if it lasted for only a few weeks. Workers did indicate that they were not as sure of their facts about sex as about other kinds of behavior. Some of the young people, especially girls, did not talk openly with their workers about their sex activities. Others, particularly boys, may well have exaggerated their conquests. It was generally agreed, however, that sex was flourishing among youth in these neighborhoods.

In several cities, there was reference to what was called "male prostitution," i.e., boys selling their services to homosexuals. This practice tended to be mentioned in connection with the most run-down neighborhoods, where there was usually a combination of weak social controls and a minimum of legitimate opportunity for earning money.

The teenage unmarried mother problem (again not limited to the lower class), seemed to be present to varying degrees in practically all of the neighborhoods represented by the workers interviewed with quite a range of attitudes toward it. One woman worker described a group of thirteen- to fifteen-year-old girls, in which the majority had babies. In another group of girls, living only a few blocks away, none had been pregnant, re-emphasizing the danger of sweeping generalizations. In some cases, the girls were said to welcome the pregnancy as a symbol of growing up, but this may have been partly bravado and conformity to what had developed as local youth mores. With the boys, there was more frequent mention of pride in having fathered a child, more so, in a few instances, if the child turned out to be a boy—a bit like medieval inheritance patterns although there was nothing for these babies to inherit. Some of the boys made quite a point of not using contraceptives, feeling that it was unmanly, while others, where social controls were stronger, were eager to prevent pregnancy. There were vivid instances of families and others descending with wrath on the boy, even of court action. Examples were given of boys who dropped out of school to work to meet financial obligations arising from the pregnancy.

The family attitudes varied from worry seemingly only about

another mouth to feed and a body to be cared for, to genuine concern about the values involved. Some families had a history of illegitimate children and here mothers were in a vulnerable position in criticizing their children for being involved in out-of-wedlock pregnancies. The sons as well as the daughters were tempted to follow the same pattern of behavior, influenced considerably by the standards of the neighborhood and of their peer group.

Increasing attention has been focused recently on the actual factors affecting illegitimacy among sublower-class and minority youth. They evidence many examples of unemployed or marginally employed men who cannot and do not function as responsible husbands and fathers. Matriarchal families are common, with grandmothers and aunts in the home, sometimes with a vaguely defined "uncle" being the only adult male. The future perceived by many of the boys for themselves does not bode well for a regularly earned, adequate and stable income, and the girls are aware of this prospect. During years when the sex urge is so strong and a quick dash toward the symbols of adulthood is so pressing, it is not surprising that large numbers of these teenagers find their own and immediate equivalent of marriage.

The babies are rarely placed for adoption. It is generally claimed that the girls and their mothers want to keep the babies but there is no real alternative; the adoption market for them is indeed small. It is probable that the girls' mothers assume most of the responsibility for the babies' care. A tragic aspect of the situation is that teenagers, still struggling not too successfully to deal with the tasks of their own adolescence, precipitate themselves into a position of responsibility for a new human being. They are rarely ready for parenthood. A worker described a group of younger teenage girls with a crop of babies, toting the infants along on their various activities, depositing the babies alongside a volleyball court, assuming that someone or other would look after them during the game. The worker felt that there was the quality of girls playing with dolls about these young mothers, and generally the statement was made that the teenagers—especially the younger ones—showed little awareness of all that is involved in being responsible for a new human being. One wonders what will happen to these babies as they grow up.

Some workers have tackled sex problems with vigor through sex

education, films about venereal disease, providing a respectable vocabulary for sex terms, meetings with parents, and pointing out vividly the potential dangers. A few took the position that they could not be effective in preventing indulgence in sexual intercourse, and therefore they stressed precautions against pregnancy. This position seemed to take on strength where social controls were stronger and the youngsters knew about instances of boys taken into court, families getting upset and angry, and other unpleasant consequences of illegitimate pregnancies.

Eliminating or even decreasing the frequency of the sex act itself, however, was presented by the workers generally as defying their best efforts. Assuming such reduction as a goal—one must recognize its many complexities and difficulties in all levels of our society —here too is a challenge for new thinking, study and experimentation. More dignity needs to be attributed to the body of the teenager, especially that of the girl. Sex needs to be understood and accepted by them in the total perspective of living, in its implications for their futures, and those of their families and the babies they bring into the world.

## D. Residuals

Associated with even the most successful work with alienated youth groups, there tended to be a hard core of residual members who were relatively uninfluenced toward more constructive functioning and attitudes. While the facts were not altogether clear, the residuals seemed to be those with the greatest personal and family pathology. Examples were mentioned of such young people using an inordinate amount of the worker's time with relatively little to show for it. This category has a large overlap with what the Group Guidance Section in Los Angeles called the "gang psycho," with practically all of his psychic and physical energy being devoted to the gang, obtaining little satisfaction in other aspects of his life. The response to the worker may be avoidance or attempts to manipulate him, while trying to undermine his influence on the rest of the group. Boys of this kind were mentioned more than girls.

As the group moved toward new and healthier developments, the residuals tended to be left behind. In some of my interviews with groups, there were boys who seemed lost or antagonistic when discussions turned toward plans for the future dealing with edu-

cation and jobs. If and when the residuals are left behind, some of them turn to younger groups, trying to stir up their hostile, fighting impulses to resurrect something like the old gang. The murder of a New York City Youth Board worker, Louis Marsh, on the evening of January 7th, 1963,[9] seems to have been committed by residuals who had been left behind by their original gang and saw Mr. Marsh being somewhat successful with a younger gang they were trying to manipulate. This double loss was too much for them and they responded in the language they knew best, violence. (It should be added that although streetwork necessitates being in dangerous situations, attacks on the workers were rarely mentioned.) The residuals tend to be sources of infection difficult to reach. Most of them need psychiatric treatment but they usually resist it. Their difficulties seem to fall into the general and perhaps vague category of character disorders.

There were varying degrees of concern for and awareness of the residuals among the agencies' personnel. Some were wisely taking the step of securing psychiatric consultation about such individuals as soon as the personality patterns became clear. There was developing the idea of exercising more authority, with the cooperation of police, probation and parole officers, and of forcing psychiatric treatment on such individuals. The position was taken that residuals are largely not amenable to the usual therapeutic approaches which build on the patient's or client's readiness for treatment; that they are a danger to themselves and others if left in the community in their present state. Usually they do something which justifies arrest, after which, it was felt, they should be incarcerated long enough to allow for treatment.

This position may be sound but there is not enough tested experience with it to be certain. The problem is serious and it, like others, calls for research and experimentation. There need to be much clearer definitions of the characteristics of the residuals, careful study to determine whether they resist streetwork regardless of the skills of the worker, the amount and duration of time devoted to the group, and other factors. The involvement of community resources needs closer scrutiny. If several agencies were to

---

[9] Described vividly by Gertrude Samuels in "Death of a Youth Worker," in *The Saturday Evening Post*, April 4, 1963. There was great interest in this tragedy on the part of streetworkers in other cities.

study their residuals, their characteristics and the methods used to deal with them in a common framework, and then pool their findings, knowledge would advance.

## Values and Psychological Characteristics

Perhaps the most dramatic value is loyalty—a good old-fashioned virtue taking the form of a troublemaker. If any of one's friends or others somehow included in the circle of loyalty (in the same group, neighborhood or housing project, or of the same racial or ethnic background) were insulted or hurt by outsiders, retaliation was required. It did not seem to matter much whether those hurt by the retaliation were the same people who perpetrated the original incident, as long as they were in the same general category. For a boy, and even in a small number of instances, a girl, to admit to fear of a fight and avoid one, was a cardinal sin. The life of that teenager would be made miserable by his peers. While driving the agency car with a group of boys who had been in a fight the day before, the worker pointed out the hazards, particularly that three of their friends were in jail. The response was, "Man, sometimes ya just gotta fight,"—a seemingly ultimate value. In another instance, the worker was trying to cool off the heated anger of a gang aroused by the shooting and beating of some of their friends by a hostile group. One boy was quoted as responding fiercely, "First we'll beat them good. *Then* we'll conversate!"

This tight combination of loyalty, retaliation and the requirement to fight is a powerful nexus. It is therefore a great tribute to community agencies that they have been able to make so marked an impact.

No human value, of course, exists in isolation. The adolescents who are not psychopathic do feel fear and do not want to get hurt or arrested, and some, alone with a worker and away from the pressures of the group, will recognize that retaliation can turn into a perpetual motion-reciprocating-action machine. But they must save face. Hence, there have been instances of a boy secretly calling the police or telling the worker about the impending fray. An interesting expression for this was, "to dime," i.e., to drop a dime in the phone to call the police. Then the group is exonerated, at least for the time being. It tried but a higher power intervened, and they

can boast and gloat over what they would have done to their enemies.

To be smart, to outwit others, to pull a clever wisecrack at someone's expense, are also highly prized attributes. All of this tends to be in a vernacular of their own, the language of their subculture, without which one does not belong. (It was difficult at times to follow our discussions. In some instances, the youngsters recognized the writer's handicap and used ordinary language. In one group a boy voluntarily took on the role of translator.) Their language is colorful and humor sprinkles much of their conversation.

Psychologically these youngsters grasp and are influenced by the concrete and the specific. General ideas like justice, honesty, industry, love, and the like are not meaningful, at least in the earlier stages of work with them. Life has taught them to be distrustful and only tangible evidence is acceptable. When the worker talks about wanting to help them, they are apt to nod vacantly. They do respond to specific help with recreational facilities, school, jobs, and with crises, such as when the worker goes into court with a boy. An executive likened this to "favors" given by politicians, suggesting a transaction between the teenagers and the worker. As another executive put it, "A golden voice and good looks won't accomplish much." Specific and meaningful alternatives to antisocial behavior must be made available.

A characteristic which is a mixture of a value and a psychological mechanism, is to project the blame for difficulties onto others. The writer asked one group of boys why they had dropped out of school. The response was that it was because they had to pass through the territory of another gang who would beat them up on the way; to a further question, they insisted that this was the only reason they became dropouts. A little later in the discussion they said that the whole problem was that the teachers did not like them and constantly picked on them. Still later, probably influenced by further questions, one boy put his finger to his head and said, "This won't work in school. Someday it might, but I can't waste my time in school."

The projection pattern applied especially to fights. As in the United Nations, no one ever admitted being the aggressor; all were acting in self-defense. The same point holds for problems with the police, who, without justified provocation, were always "picking

on them," as the adolescents described the situation. Progress was shown by some groups in comments such as, "The cops are needed and have a job to do," and, "Some cops are O.K." Helping the youngsters get perspective on their projections and take more responsibility for their own behavior was a major aim of the workers. Someone suggested that it was like peeling the layers off an artichoke to get at the heart.

Low self-esteem is pathetically characteristic of the youngsters, and was consistently talked about by the workers. One boy, probably sixteen years old and the indigenous leader of his group, marched around the room, swaggering and grimacing, saying, "I'm the President," (which he was, of the group); "I'm great." Then a little later after he had won some games of ping-pong and pool, with the same antics complained, "Why can't nobody beat me!" This behavior suggested the young child trying to establish his sense of an adequate self. It was as though human worth depended on constant demonstration of achievement in whatever realm happened to be important.

Other values could be presented, but it is well to move on to what seems to be the core value challenge. On the centuries-old free will-determinism issue, many of these youngsters have, perhaps without being conscious of it, taken the position that the areas in which choice can be exercised, in which free and intelligent decisions can be made and followed, are very small. They are, for the most part, controlled and driven by circumstances, conditions, values and feelings, without sufficient opportunities for intelligently thinking about choices and values, which is the essence of human dignity. They are hemmed in by the limitations of their families and neighborhoods, the walls of lack of legitimate opportunity, prejudice, community indifference, and the congeries of the values which are a defense against an all but hopeless situation. The great decisions to be made about marriage, education, work, religion, community commitments and citizenship, recreational interests and friendships, largely get made for them. The tragic need is for social, economic and political changes and for help on a more intimate level so that these youngsters can learn to respect themselves, thereby learning to respect others, and to develop what is the right of all people, the opportunity to make intelligent decisions and to be ready to live with their consequences.

## CHAPTER THREE

THE AGENCIES WORKING with hostile youth groups have complex programs and their patterns are far from fitting in a standard mold. While their methods have common features, as do many of the problems in the youngsters they serve, the differences among the agencies are marked.

# the agencies and their

# programs

**Patterns of Organization and Sources of Funds**

A. City-Wide Public Agencies

A clear example of this category is the New York City Youth Board, which derives its support from the City and the State. At the time of the visit, there were 187 streetworkers in twenty-eight neighborhoods. Emphasis was placed on coordinated services, with a staff of six to nine streetworkers along with a community organizer and a caseworker assigned to each area. The Youth Board program includes a wide variety of services devoted to the sub-lower class, and it is the largest agency of its kind in the country. To supplement its own services, it has contractual arrangements with other agencies.

The Youth Activities Bureau in Boston operates out of the Mayor's office and it served five areas with high delinquency rates, with its major budget of $76,000 provided equally by the City and the State (via the Massachusetts Youth Service Board). It did receive small donations from other sources for work in additional areas. Some settlement houses in Boston were also providing small

amounts of this type of service, but the Youth Activities Bureau, with its six streetworkers, a supervisor and an executive, was carrying the biggest part of the load of working with hostile youth groups—a modest, even meager, number of workers for a city of Boston's size.

The Los Angeles Group Guidance Section of the Probation Department is also a much smaller operation than the Youth Board in New York, with less varied programs, but its funds are derived primarily from taxes. In connection with research being conducted by the Youth Studies Center of the University of Southern California with Ford Foundation funds, the Group Guidance Section budget was enhanced to employ more workers in an experimental area. It had fifteen workers.

The Roving Leader Program of the District of Columbia Recreation Department serves the District, and it had eleven workers on the streets, frequently making use of the facilities of the Recreation Department. It was the only agency among those visited which was developed in a recreation department. It resembled in structure the Group Guidance Section in Los Angeles in that it was developed as an extension of an existing agency, in contrast with the Youth Board in New York and the Youth Activities Bureau in Boston, agencies specially created for working with groups of alienated youngsters.

The Mobilization for Youth is not city-wide but operates in a selected segment of the lower East Side of Manhattan; it's supported by funds from a variety of sources, including the National Institute of Mental Health, the President's Committee on Juvenile Delinquency and Youth Crime, the Ford Foundation and New York City. Contrary to the usual pattern, it pays the Youth Board to work with gangs in its area. Mobilization is an imaginative program, with major emphasis on the opportunity-blockage theory. It runs small businesses to give youth work experience, under certain conditions it shares with employers the payment of young people's wages, it provides a coffee house (more are to come) with an atmosphere congenial to somewhat sophisticated youth as a base for various services, it provides vocational guidance and has various other activities in its program. Work with hostile youth groups on the streets is not as central for Mobilization as it is for the other agencies considered in this chapter.

B. Combined Public and Voluntary Sources of Funds

The clearest example of this combination of sources is the Crime Prevention Association in Philadelphia. State and city funds are available, as well as those from voluntary sources. It had thirty-five to forty workers, both full and part-time. It is free to move its services to any area in Philadelphia where group violence develops, and may place a worker in a neighborhood served by another agency if requested to do so by that agency, although a few settlements have their own programs of this type. An unusual feature of the Crime Prevention Association is that in some respects it is responsible to the Youth Conservation Service of the Department of Welfare, which is the vehicle through which the Crime Prevention Association receives some of its funds.

The practice of using public funds to purchase services for experimental projects with alienated youth groups from voluntary agencies seemed to be in the developmental stage in the Los Angeles area.

C. Voluntary and City-Wide

The only example encountered in this study of a city-wide program supported by voluntary funds was the Neighborhood Service Organization in Detroit. It has a many-sided program, with about thirty-five percent of its budget, or $70,000, devoted to what it calls Special Services to Youth; it was working with about twenty youth groups. It cooperated with the YMCA and other agencies so that additional groups were served. A somewhat unusual feature of this agency is that its beginning point of contact with the groups frequently is the Detroit Police Department (Youth Bureau and Women's Division). When the police have picked up youngsters for infractions of the law, they frequently call on the Neighborhood Service Organization to work with the groups.

D. Voluntary—not City-Wide

This category includes the majority of the agencies visited. The larger ones were in Chicago: the Chicago Youth Centers, the Chicago YMCA, and the Youth Development Project of the Chicago Boys Clubs. Foundations and other non-tax sources provided their funds. Smaller programs were being advanced in the Chicago Com-

mons, the Neighborhood Service Organization, and other settlement houses. For a time this work was coordinated by Dr. Catherine V. Richards, and the experience is described in *Breaking Through Barriers*,[1] but this arrangement was modified when the special funds for it were terminated. Judging from numerous comments, there were substantial advantages in the availability of this coordination, which included training and consultation.

In other cities, there were agencies operating in one or a few neighborhoods. Some of these agencies, such as Special Services to Groups in Los Angeles, specialized in work with alienated youth groups. Others, such as Telegraph Hill in San Francisco, included this work along with more general settlement house functions.

### E. Special Patterns

United Youth in Cleveland had a coordinator based in the Welfare Federation, and it hired and paid part-time workers, with other full-time jobs, each of whom was based in one of the existing group service agencies and was supervised by a member of its staff. The budget for the payment of these workers was $28,000, a surprisingly small amount to deal with problems so extensive and complex. The Cleveland arrangement had the advantage of regular training sessions for the workers, and a more coordinated approach to other agencies. The part-time worker aspect of the situation was generally recognized as an obstacle. It limited work with schools during the day and contacts with the youngsters, their families and other agencies because workers were busy elsewhere during the usual working hours.

Other types of programs merit attention. The Neighborhood Youth Association in Los Angeles, unlike most of the other agencies visited, formed groups out of youngsters individually referred to it, instead of working with existing formations. The referrals were largely from schools, and probation and police departments. The advantages seen by the agency in this approach were that they might thereby reach problem youngsters at an earlier age, more information tended to be available, they could select others for the group who would be helpful to the referred youngster, and they could reach the isolated and others whose peer relationships were

---

[1] *Breaking Through Barriers* (Welfare Council of Metropolitan Chicago [1960]).

superficial.[2] The groups are kept small so that intensive work can be done with each member.

A similar approach in that groups are formed by the agency among troubled youngsters referred by junior high schools is being tried by the Atlantic Street Center in Seattle (not visited by writer; information was provided by the executive) under a grant from the National Institute of Mental Health. An elaborate research program is tied into the service. Like the Los Angeles agency, the Atlantic Street Center concentrates on youngsters who have acute problems, many of whom are highly vulnerable to delinquency. The groups were limited to nine members to make possible intensive work with each; emphasis was on prevention.

An unusual, if not unique, program was applied by Youth for Service in San Francisco. It was originated by the American Friends Service Committee, but later became an independent agency. It built upon the service motivation in groups of hostile youngsters. Through the Welfare Department, or from other sources, names of older people living under difficult conditions were secured and the gang boys in small groups would clean up or paint their apartments. Other projects involved service to a rehabilitation center, building bridges for Indians, and the like. The boys were called for and driven home, and were given a free lunch prepared by volunteers.

In view of what is generally known about the values of these youngsters, it was surprising to find them responding to an altruistic appeal. Yet the staff said that they sometimes had more boys interested than there were suitable projects. The explanation suggested is that these boys receive an increased feeling of significance through being able to serve others.

In addition to these projects, Youth for Service had a small number of streetworkers, a council of representatives of gangs, and other activities.

---

2 This program is in some respects similar to that of the Department of Neighborhood Clubs of Boston Children's Services, although the latter emphasizes more the isolated youngster, and works with somewhat younger children.

## Comments

In the face of this amazing variety of organizational patterns and programs, it is difficult to formulate specific recommendations as to which lend themselves best to the designated service tasks. Clear evidence is not available to show that whatever advantages or disadvantages exist are necessarily related to the structure of the agency. Many other variables operate. Nevertheless, some general principles do seem reasonable.

Financial stability and adequacy are essential. Some of the agencies visited were so harried by worries about finances that their executives, and to a lesser extent the whole staff, were devoting much of their physical and psychic energies to dealing with their hand-to-mouth existence. Such was their uncertainty about the future that one cannot help wondering whether they could approach the youngsters with the emotional security essential for this kind of work. In some instances, the voluntary agencies were, for this part of their programs, either not firmly established in, or were on the margins of, the Community Fund or United Fund. Where foundation or federal grants supported the programs, there were the inevitable time limitations, perhaps five or six years, and what was to happen after the deadline was a big question mark. Furthermore, most of these grants entailed evaluation requirements, so that agencies were under pressure not only to move ahead quickly with their action and research programs, but also to show favorable achievements at a pace which may be unrealistic, and which could interfere with the slow and thoughtful planning which should be characteristic of services designed to meet infinitely complex problems. Even in some of the agencies supported out of tax funds, there was a stepchild-like quality to their position.

The idea has been advanced that the status of agencies often reflects that of the people they serve, and it seems to have striking application to many of the agencies included in this study. The youth, their families and their sublower-class neighborhoods, have been largely by-passed by the advancement of affluence and its symbols, by the best in education and culture, and generally by what is regarded as good and desirable in our society. The fact that these agencies are sincerely and vigorously trying to redress the

balance helps to restore faith in human decency, but the further fact that so many of them are supported left-handedly and impermanently imparts a bitter taste. The needs to be met are enormous, and stability and security in the agencies are desperately required for work with people whose lives are dramatically unstable and insecure.

How can this debilitating condition be changed? The general situation in the voluntary field is that whatever greater amounts, if any, are raised annually by Community Fund and United Fund campaigns barely meet the rising costs of existing agencies and programs; when new and expanding services are proposed, the response is apt to be to ask which of the current beneficiaries should be cut off to provide the money.

There has been a growing trend in the voluntary agencies to serve the middle class, softened somewhat by charging increased fees for services. Nevertheless, a basic policy question is whether voluntary social services should continue to move away from their historic tradition of concentrating on the poor. To be sure, the middle class is more verbal and receptive to the structure of the services, but there is the danger of being seduced by one's methods into selecting clients who respond better to them, without regard to the massive and greater problems of the sublower class. It is reassuring that some agencies have moved out to the poor and have been trying to develop methods which work with them, but not nearly enough of them are doing so.

However, even if the voluntary funds were redistributed in favor of the poor, the funds thereby made available could not be adequate. Public funds from tax sources are required. Cities and states in some instances (New York, Boston, Los Angeles, Philadelphia, Washington, etc.) are providing for work with alienated youth groups but usually to an inadequate extent; the outlook for more from these sources is not too bright. The plan which seems to hold the greatest hope would be in the pattern of what is done in child welfare and other services on a national level, i.e., for the federal government to make the necessary funds available, with the states and cities assuming the responsibility of supplying a fair percentage of the total. The grants by the President's Committee on Juvenile Delinquency and Youth Crime have been used to stimulate new kinds of programs, research and training; there is much to be said for

this approach, especially with the limited funds available. What is proposed here, however, is that larger amounts be given to existing agencies working with groups of delinquent or anti-social youth. If no suitable agency exists in some communities, responsible people could be stimulated to create one. These grants could go to public and voluntary agencies, and there are many precedents for both.

Estimates have been made that streetwork costs from $200 to $600 annually for each youngster, depending on the intensity of the service. This is little enough to pay for work that genuinely reaches them and often their families, and which can open many doors to a better future.

Moving away from finances, other principles command attention. Whether the program evolves in an agency specialized for work with alienated youth groups, or in one carrying out additional functions, there needs to be a firm and vital commitment to sub-lower-class youth. In a larger agency, with other responsibilities predominating, there is the danger, not just speculative, of the streetwork program taking on the minority and lower-class status of the people it serves. Furthermore, imaginativeness, flexibility and integrity are essential. The methods must be ready to move in whatever directions the problems require, with an honest readiness to examine failures, often rich sources of learning. The agency should have the strength to resist doing a "snow job," as the youngsters say, about the effectiveness of the service, even under the realistic pressures to sell itself so that it can secure the needed funds.

### Selection of Groups to Be Served

In all of the cities the need for streetwork seemed to be greater than the resources, and difficult decisions had to be made about priorities. It was gratifying to find that practically all of the agencies did a study of each individual group and its background before reaching a decision.

Several of the agencies delegated assignments on an area basis, with the workers serving whatever suitable groups existed in that area. The rationale was that this practice led to less feeling of exclusive possession of the worker by each group, but the net result

may make little difference. The assignment to a specific group usually involves work with the area and the most common practice was to assign workers to two or more groups. Furthermore, the feeling of "possessing" the worker has implications for identification with him, which is one of the primary dynamics for change. The more realistic deciding factors would seem to be the number of people with whom the worker should have contacts, how intense the associations should be, and the nature of the problems in question in relation to all those claiming attention.

- The agencies varied in the precision with which they had formulated criteria for the guidance of decisions about service. Some were rather general; others more specific. Practically all the agencies emphasized as justifying the service such behavior as fighting, trouble with the law, disruption of the community, and additionally, requests, even pressures, from police, teachers, and community leaders. Fortunately, most of the agencies had goals which went beyond merely stopping violence and other gross forms of delinquency, yet the latter were most frequently cited as a basis for a decision to provide service. The majority of the agencies seemed to be functioning where they were most needed.

Another condition was that the group not be associated with another agency, unless the latter asked for help via a streetworker. The age range often was twelve to eighteen years at the time of intake, although some expressed reservations about starting with youngsters above sixteen. Inter-group tensions, population movement and social breakdown in housing projects were cited as justifying service.

Other criteria mentioned by some were that the group not be too large or that a workable subgroup within it be available, and that it live in not too spread-out an area, although it was repeatedly mentioned that those who moved away usually returned to the old hangouts for a period. The group might be selected because of its influential position in the neighborhood, and it should be reachable. In practically all agencies, it was the practice to develop some relationship with older gang members whose cooperation would forward the work, and with community people in key spots relative to the group served.

As was indicated earlier, girls were much less concentrated on than boys. In some instances, there was a prevention orientation

in which younger, vulnerable children were selected, usually involving agency formation of a group. Staff limitations at times made it necessary to put a group on a waiting list, but frequently some contact was initiated. The design of research programs usually incorporated methods of determining whom to serve. An interesting and not altogether rare situation involved unserved groups misbehaving obviously in order to secure a worker. They might get into conflict with a served group to force the agency to give them one.

Rather rarely mentioned were reasons for deciding not to serve a group. Indicated by only a few were the following:

1) Extreme pathology in several members, such as strong sadistic tendencies, character disorders, etc.

2) Gang too old, leaving little time for service before the usual disintegration of the group which tends to occur, added to the point that workers have found older teenagers less receptive.

3) Dope addicts, because of the fear that they would use the group to influence others to turn to serious drugs. This was not predominant among the agencies.

4) Youngsters coming from families in which sex is out of control (mentioned by a psychiatric consultant) who would unduly stimulate the group in this direction. Cited by the same psychiatrist were the mentally defective delinquents.

5) Youngsters who do not need this relatively intensive and expensive service. An escapade can mislead a community into assuming consistent delinquency exists when the problem may be circumstantial and temporary. The temptation to yield to a request for service to this type of group is reinforced by the way the youngsters and their families respond to the worker, in contrast with slower, more suspicious and less cooperative responses from teenagers and their families with more serious problems.

### The Contacts

One of the contributions of streetwork has been to take the ideas of working with all relevant people and the meaningful coordination of services out of the realm of pious resolution into that of practiced reality. The urgent and dramatic needs of the youngsters make any lesser approach futile.

## A. Families

The agencies varied in the emphasis, amount of attention and level of skills which were devoted to the families of the youngsters, but all recognized the importance of relating to them. In view of the rebelliousness of adolescents and their strivings for independence, care must be exercised in how, when and under what conditions the worker approaches parents. A further complication is that hostile adolescents often express strong negative feelings about their parents, especially under the pressures of familial conflicts, which occur frequently. The worker needs insight and skill to understand and help with the other side of the ambivalence, the positive feelings toward their families on the part of the teenagers and the strong need to feel that there is good in the people who brought them into the world and who, however inadequately, have cared for them. There is usually a comparable duality of feelings in the parents.

As the relationship with the worker develops, a strong element of parent substitute is generated. This can easily lead to unfavorable comparisons with the real parents, and maturity is required to save the worker from taking so much satisfaction from his apparent success that he may fail to see that strengthening the family, rather than supplanting it, should be his goal.

Some agencies focused clearly on helping the parents to become more adequate, with the worker almost assuming a teaching function, and offering them great support. They were approached in the spirit of sharing with the worker the concern about the teenagers' welfare.

While all agencies stressed work with families, the desirable level of workers' knowledge and skill was far from universally present. This was one of the areas in which many of the workers said they would like further training.

Some youngsters have families so weak that little seems possible in the way of work with them. The workers then find it necessary to substitute for the parents in a somewhat literal sense, to sign report cards, to get the boys up in the morning, to suggest how they should dress and to do other things which are ordinarily handled by parents.

## B. Schools

The school is recognized by many of the alienated young people as the path to a better future, but one that is forced on them, intrinsically lacks appeal to many of them. It usually has been the scene of frustrations and failures. Many of these youth become the much talked-about dropouts. In some instances, schools have found them so difficult that they became "pushouts." But many efforts are being made to find ways of making educational experiences meaningful to these youngsters, some within and others outside of school buildings, and the streetworker is often essential if these innovations are to influence the hardest to reach.

Many examples were given by the workers of success in helping the youngsters get back into school. This is a many-sided task. Youth must be motivated to give up what they regard as important, to exchange hanging around the streets, for what, as one of them put it, is "wasting my time in school." This is a transformation of behavior and values which requires endless patience, faith and skill to achieve. It also means finding a school program which makes some sense to the youngsters, and interpreting their personalities and problems to the school officials who often have all they can do to provide satisfactory education for the more tractable youngsters. It may involve helping to provide a place congenial for study, since the homes do not frequently lend themselves to it, and individual tutoring. Work with parents is apt to be involved. Crises develop which are touch-and-go, and the worker's support is crucial.

If a youngster has been out of school a long time and his educational history was very negative, the worker may fail. Several reported this situation, and how to help such youth move toward healthy adulthood became a soul-searching problem. Enlistment in the armed services or a period of some kind of work which would convince the teenager of the value of resuming his education were mentioned as alternatives. The pressure for a high school diploma is so great these days that those who do not obtain it are unfortunately rather publicly labeled as failures. The expressions on their faces as this issue was discussed with them were haunting. They were up against what they regarded as antagonistic and powerful forces which were throwing them onto the junk heap, perhaps —pardon the pun—onto the junkie heap.

## C. Securing Psychiatric Help

The agencies varied as to whether they made it a practice to secure psychiatric consultation for the workers about difficult individual problems. It is highly significant that those who did take
advantage of psychiatric consultation universally said that it was
helpful. It would be very desirable for all agencies working with
groups of troubled youth to arrange for it. Acute individual pathology is far from rare among these groups, and a high level of diagnostic skill is needed to assess each situation. This is not to deny
the powerful impact of social pathology, but individuals differ in
their reactions and in their capacities to master great tensions. Unfortunately, some agencies have chosen to disregard psychody-
namics and psychopathology, and to put all of their professional
eggs into the sociological basket. The consistent testimony of
agency people receiving psychiatric consultation should be convinc-
ing evidence of its helpfulness.

One difficulty was mentioned by some—not all—streetworkers,
i.e., the tendency on the part of some psychiatrists to overlook or
belittle the differences between their usual middle-class patients
and the sublower-class people served by the streetworkers, placing
upon the latter the whole burden of translating—and it is a real
translation—the consultation into the language, mores, behavior
and values of a very different social class. Fortunately, some psychiatrists had the point of view which motivated them to take the
trouble to learn about the characteristics of the lower class.[3]

Moving from consultation to psychiatric treatment for sublower-
class youth, the picture is bleak. Even if the herculean efforts to
prepare a youngster for treatment were successful, the repeated
story, with only a few exceptions, was that the clinics had long
waiting lists, with months before this referral could be reached. The
transaction usually ended at that point. It was difficult enough for
the youth to overcome his feelings about going to a "head
shrinker," but to wait an indefinite or long period was just too much.
There were attempts to deal with this gap in new ways. The New
York City Youth Board was trying to develop a plan whereby psychiatrists would move out to the youngsters and their families. An

---

[3] For a study of the class orientation of psychiatry see August B. Hollingshead and Frederick C. Redlich, *Social Class and Mental Illness* (New
York: John Wiley & Sons, 1958).

impressive program in Chicago is described in *Sociological and Psychiatric Aspects of a Street Corner Group*,[4] a project of the Institute for Juvenile Research. It was limited to one group, but the plan of the psychiatrists' building on relationships established by the streetworker and offering treatment in the neighborhood has possibilities.

Realistically, however, in view of the number of psychiatrists in relation to those needing treatment, consultation with streetworkers may well be the only practical course. Our society does not seem ready to compensate psychiatrists enough to attract them in large numbers to treat the sublower class. Sharpening the diagnostic awareness and skills of the streetworkers through consultation with psychiatrists may be all that can be expected.

In securing casework services, too, the workers rather consistently reported waiting lists and other factors which made intensive and skilled casework service relatively unavailable. Family and children's agencies were said to be insufficiently willing to adapt their approaches and make the required heavy investment of the workers' time in the sublower class. There were some heartening exceptions among the voluntary agencies, and situations in which public welfare agencies were conducting programs involving trained, skilled caseworkers. Again, they are exceptions and the gaps are large. It is sad to see social work neglecting the poor.

The streetwork agencies which have their own caseworkers are fortunate, but they usually do not make up for the services which should be available in the family and child welfare fields.

## D. Police

There was a time when relations with the police was the hottest issue among streetworkers. Now the picture varies, and many instances were cited of excellent relationships. The quality of leadership in the police departments and in the agencies seemed to be the crucial factor. Reports were highly favorable on sections of the police departments, such as Juvenile Aid Bureau, Youth Bureau, etc. devoted to youth. The officer on the beat often was said to be less understanding and cooperative, but the situation varied with the individual. Instances were cited of such officers making a point

---

[4] Solomon Kobrin and Brahm Baittle, *Sociological and Psychiatric Aspects of a Street Corner Group* (Children's Bureau [1962]).

of visiting the places where the youth met to get acquainted with them under congenial conditions. It is unfortunate to have the contacts between police and the young people limited to times of conflict, which is all too often the case. There were many examples of joint participation by police and agency representatives in community committees and organizations.

But one must realistically recognize some built-in tensions arising out of differences in functions and points of view. The job of the police is to enforce the law and apprehend those who break it, not to rehabilitate. The streetworker shares the concern about the law and the community's protection, but he is vitally concerned with rehabilitation. Working so hard on the establishment of a trusting relationship with anti-social teenagers, he is wary of being asked to be a stool pigeon for the police. Many streetworkers grew up in neighborhoods like the ones in which they work, and it is not easy for them to attain perspective on their earlier attitudes toward the police. There were occasions during the writer's interviews when there seemed to be an unhealthy satisfaction on the part of the worker in the hostility which the teenagers expressed toward the police. Unfortunately, there were enough examples of police brutality and prejudice against minority groups to make it much more difficult for both youth and workers to achieve a healthy attitude.

The police, even those designated to work with youth, tended to be negative toward gangs, their leaders, and efforts to mediate conflicts between gang representatives; they evidenced suspicion of agencies which deal sympathetically with these realities. It is understandable that the police be keenly aware of how these groups seem to support their members in breaking the law and therefore the obvious conclusion is reached that the groups should be destroyed and their leadership undermined. What is overlooked is the powerful set of needs served by such groups and the very real possibility that suppression will drive them underground, or that individual members could become more of a problem to themselves and society if they were deprived of the group.

Perhaps even more basic is the view of human nature which seems to be held by some police. People tend to get divided into good and bad, and the position is taken that once bad, always bad. The streetworker, on the other hand, is committed to the validity

of the potentiality for constructive change, and the conflict in opinion is a frequent irritant between the two representatives of the community.

These are vivid examples of the many situations in our society in which a degree of conflict is inevitable, examples which can be utilized constructively. One approach is to emphasize the common goal. Both community institutions want obedience to the law. Streetwork agencies stress this point. They ask their workers to make clear to the adolescents that they are on the side of the law and that in the long run this will be helpful to the teenagers. If the workers and the police are clear about each other's functions and there is mutual respect, good cooperation can be attained. In view of the strong hostility most of these teenagers feel toward the police, a healthy relationship between the workers and the police is crucial.

## E. Courts and Probation Officers

The workers went frequently to court when youngsters in their groups were arrested. In many instances, the judges welcomed their testimony, and examples were cited of heavy reliance on the workers' judgment about the disposition of the case. There were a few situations in which the workers were assigned the probation function, which seems to be a confusion of roles. It is better to have a probation officer take on that responsibility, and to develop a cooperative relationship between him and the streetworker, a condition that seemed to obtain in the majority of instances.

A delicate issue is involved in the position taken by the worker in court. The youngster is apt to pressure him to try to persuade the judge to free him with no punishment. Some workers were clear and helpful in pointing out that if one breaks the law, he must face the consequences. The worker is present to provide information about the teenager which might be helpful to the judge and to stand by the boy through a difficult experience, not to try to manipulate the court. If he thought that going to a training school would be damaging to the youth, he usually felt free to say so to the judge.

## F. Other Contacts

The worker often dealt with employment agencies, potential employers, hospitals, and others. There seemed to be a gratifying readiness to call upon whatever resources were needed. These contacts required a heavy investment of the worker's time, and they are telling arguments for keeping the group and individual assignments of the worker down to manageable proportions.

### Problems of Strategy

With the insufficiency of finances and workers, the administrations of these agencies face difficult questions about the distribution of their services. Should they concentrate on limited areas or move out to whatever parts of the city need service, thereby thinning out the service? It was learned long ago that to work with one group when it is in close contact or conflict with others, creates an imbalance, somewhat like unilateral disarmament. If the served group is persuaded to give up fighting, the members are apt to be victimized by the others. Where such groups are in close contact, work with all of them is indicated, which is likely to mean that other parts of the city are neglected.

The duration and depth of the work with each group presents another troubling question and involves the goals of the agency. After meeting with one group when service to it had been terminated, the writer suggested to the worker and the supervisor that the boys still had serious problems. They agreed but made the point that this group was no longer fighting and that the agency felt pressure to place its workers where fighting occurs. This is not an unreasonable position, but it does mean that the goals of the agency must be modified in the direction of more modest expectations in such areas as school adjustment, the ability to hold a job, sexual behavior and other non-aggressive activities.

Another recurring dilemma is the matter of prevention. Why wait until the youngsters are in their teens, well launched on their anti-social careers? Why not work with them at a younger stage when they are probably more open to influence? Some—but not many—agencies do this, but with resources so limited, it means that teenagers are thereby neglected. In neighborhoods where teen-

age delinquency is prevalent and visible, it has an impact on younger children, and work with the latter is therefore more difficult. A good argument can be made both ways on this issue.

The only satisfactory solution to these and other questions is to increase the financial and other resources of the agencies. They have a wonderful story to tell about the rehabilitation of young people, a story on which they have so much information. They need to be bolder in making the larger communities, especially people in policy-making positions, aware of the seriousness of the problems and of what is required to deal effectively with them. Much could be accomplished if the American people were aroused to the urgent needs.

## CHAPTER FOUR

AN ENORMOUS AMOUNT of work and goodly sums of money are going into group services to alienated youth, and questions are raised on all sides about its effectiveness. Unfortunately, it is about as difficult and complicated to answer these questions satisfactorily as it is to achieve desired changes in the young people. It is reas-

# achievements

suring that an increasing amount of research is being done on these programs and it will be considered in a later chapter. What are presented here are the judgments of the people interviewed.

There is the immediate issue of bias. All of us have the need to succeed and are tempted to color the results accordingly. There is no way to eliminate this tendency but certain factors keep it under control. In this part of the interviews, agency people were urged to respond, not in terms of their aspirations—pie in the sky, —but rather with what their experience realistically supports in reference to changes which actually occur in their group members. That they took this point seriously is attested to by their consistent citation of failures as well as successes. There were differences among the workers on what could be called an optimism-pessimism dimension, but it never went so far as to claim complete success or failure. It took the form of differing on how much achievement or lack of it should be claimed, but there was a surprising amount of consistency about the areas in which achievements can be expected. In graphic terms, the curves went up and down at about the same points, but they varied in how much up or down they went. The exceptions were largely accounted for by external conditions, e.g., there was the greatest discouragement about helping young people find jobs in Detroit, where unemployment was high.

A balancing factor was introduced by interviewing people not employed by these agencies, yet in a position to assess their work —school officials, judges, police, probation officers, and others. Here too, there was relative consistency with the judgments of the streetworkers, with sometimes greater optimism about achievements. The differences tended to be about methods, as illustrated by the suspiciousness of many police about work with gangs, and their plea for "stronger" action by the streetworkers.

The writer had the additional advantages of not being in any way associated with the sources of the agencies' funds, of being sincerely interested in what they were doing, and of approaching them in the context of adding to the knowledge and experience needed for greater effectiveness. A final and potent point is that most of these workers tend to care so much about the young people they serve, that forces which block achievement get full attention. Many presented the skill of the worker as primary.

Recognizing that complete objectivity is not here—or possibly anywhere—available, we are ready for what was claimed in the way of success. An open question was asked first about the factors which affect success and failure. It drew quite a response.

### Factors Affecting Success

One such aggregation included community conditions. Success was regarded as blocked or hampered by rapid population changes, urban renewal when it resulted in gang members moving into new areas and producing friction with older residents, large housing projects which led to anonymity for the youngsters, poor adult models, lack of suitable services, community attitudes which were extreme in the sense either of supporting anti-social attitudes or of branding a group of youth as bad and treating them accordingly, uncooperative police (considerable improvement was reported in most of the cities), and insufficient suitable opportunities for these young people in the realms of education and employment.

The familial attitudes were repeatedly stated to be crucial. They ranged from being concerned about the youth and welcoming the help of the agency, to indifference. There were many instances in which the family was so weak and riddled with problems that the worker learned to have low expectations of cooperation. Yet there

were surprises, i.e., some youngsters from such families did change constructively.

Another set of elements was in the youth. If seriously pathological members had attained positions of leadership in the group, the worker's influence tended to be nullified. He might be able to reach healthier members and to encourage some of them to become leaders, but this was difficult. Intelligence was mentioned by several, with the subnormal youth being more difficult to influence. While there was some dissension about age, the predominant opinion was that better results were achieved in the earlier rather than in the later teen years, and that older youth sometimes tried to undermine the worker's efforts with the younger ones, although there were instances to the contrary. Mentioned with some frequency were young people returning to their old haunts from training schools and trying to reconstruct the old gang in the old pattern. The worker had to be alert to reinforce whatever constructive changes had occurred and to attempt to move the returnee along in their direction. If the boy had been a leader of the group and had hardened in his delinquent tendencies while in the training school, he would look upon the worker as a foe rather than a helper. A final variable was the morale of the young people. If they had gone so far down the anti-social road as to have lost a sense of hope and purpose about becoming healthy adults, achievements with them were retarded.

A last set of factors dealt with the worker, the agency and community resources. A high level of skill, good supervision, a reasonable work load and access to needed services were regarded as conducive to effective work. Abiding faith in the young people was rated as crucial.

None of the above factors in isolation were regarded as final determinants. The point of view tended to be rather that each had some impact, and that a combination of several negative ones made the success of the worker dubious.

### The Results

The above factors affecting success were spontaneous responses. Next, a framework of goals was presented so that the responses could be grouped:

## A. Public behavior [1]

This entails the engagement of the group or a large part of it in fights, theft or vandalism. The question was how succesful the worker and the agency had been in modifying or eliminating this kind of behavior.

This goal was consistently reported as the area of greatest achievement. While much more needs to be done over and beyond stopping public misbehavior, its importance should not be underrated. Each instance of the prevention of damage to property and the hurting, even killing, of people is an achievement of great value. With each such episode, there are apt to be the further consequences of arrest and incarceration, which have serious implications for the youth and their futures. A goodly number of them, if they can be helped through the turbulence of adolescence, may well settle down to a more regulated and law-abiding adulthood. But a dramatic conflict with the law can set forces in motion which portend a dismal future.

Agencies varied in the frequency of contact between the workers and the youngsters, but practically all emphasized intensive work before, during and after crises. This is a great aid in work with volatile teenagers; incidents can develop rapidly. The worker has a steadying influence, sifting wild rumors, pointing out consequences, urging that police be asked to handle the situation when appropriate, and making clear that his concern for this group of boys and others who might be hurt and get into trouble would make it necessary for him to call the police if they persisted.

Taking weapons away from the teenagers was common practice. At one agency, during a discussion of achievements, a worker referred to a drawer full of weapons—some very formidable—and with great earnestness urged that their presence in the drawer meant that they could not hurt anyone. As a supervisor and the writer were leaving a worker in the Crime Prevention Association in Philadelphia, he mentioned that before going home—it was late

---

[1] The formulation of the goal of public behavior, and the one that follows, private behavior, is taken from an article by David M. Austin, "Goals for Gang Workers," in *Social Work,* Vol. II, No. 4, October, 1957. It is noteworthy that my findings support what he wrote about achievements in relation to the two goals. My third and fourth goals were not dealt with in his article.

in the evening—he had to get a gun away from a boy. His tone was casual, suggesting nothing unusual about his task.

Probably one significant reason why decreases in public delinquent behavior are relatively achievable is that the consequences tend to be quick, visible and in terms which the youth understand. In this category are injuries, arrest, and retaliation by the enemy groups. Unfortunate results in relation to other kinds of behavior, such as drinking, sex, and the use of drugs, are not so immediate and clear to the teenagers.

The worker faces the challenge of helping to provide satisfactory substitutes for the excitement of fighting, stealing and vandalism. His resources are group programs which meet important needs, counseling, help with school and jobs, and a new image of the group in the community. It would not be psychologically meaningful or sound to expect these young people to give up behavior and attitudes which mean a lot to them without providing satisfactory alternatives, a difficult task. Fighting has not stopped, but its large scale and more destructive forms have decreased.

## B.  Private Behavior

Private misbehavior includes sex, and the use of drugs and drinking. There seem to have been tendencies toward making sexual activity less of a group enterprise, while drinking was done quite publicly in many instances. The use of drugs was frequently private, but with notable exceptions. Regardless of such trends, the question here is how effective the workers and others thought they were.

While the responses were far from completely negative in this area, they were mostly discouraging. The resistances to change in relation to sex, drugs and alcohol seemed to be as strong, if not stronger, in the youth than those to other kinds of change. They are accessible escapes from drab and frustrating living, and they provide exciting enjoyment. They also symbolize adulthood.

Whatever successes were reported were usually linked to other changes, such as obtaining a good job, improved family relationships, developing ability and interest in athletics, strong identification with the worker, and the like. The low batting average of success indicates that new knowledge and methods are needed.

## C. Interpersonal Relations

"Interpersonal relations" means how the youth treat each other, whether they show concern about the misfortunes of their fellows, pleasure in their good fortune, and other forms of what is generally regarded as highly socialized and mature behavior. Again the focus is on how much the worker is able to achieve.

The workers found that the young people are at different levels at the beginning of the work. In some instances loyalty to each other went well beyond defense and attack against enemies, with a kind of cameraderie that was impressive. Many, however, tended to show lack of trust in each other, and callousness in their relationships. "Ranking" (teasing, wise-cracking, belittling each other) was very common. This and similar forms of behavior are widely found among middle-class youth and even adults, but it seems to be more intense and harsh among sub-lower class teenagers, who often are very clever at it.

The group work method has rich contributions to make toward improved interpersonal relations. After the worker becomes trusted and liked by the members, and shows active concern about what happens to every one of them, there often is a shift, over a period of time, in their attitudes and behavior toward each other. Time, patience, devotion and skill are essential, but many workers reported substantial changes. Only a few of the many examples given will be cited.

The ridicule of a mentally ill boy in one group decreased. Another held a big party to celebrate the graduation from high school of one of their members who had encountered educational difficulties. Some boys asked for advice on how to behave on dates. Examples were given of groups calling for a member to get him to school or to a job. An elderly woman offered some money to boys in the Youth for Service program in San Francisco for work in her home, and they politely refused it. Their understanding was that the work was voluntary service, and they said so. Instances were described of older adolescents helping with recreation for younger children.

In our legitimate interest in tangible goals like stopping violence and delinquency, and promoting school attendance and jobs, there is the danger of overlooking or slighting the less obvious goal of

helping these young people experience more satisfying and mature relationships. The worker often provides their first opportunity to enjoy in a meaningful way the richness and depth of trusting and considerate interdependence with their fellows. This theme does not ring the tocsin of public relations and fund raising, nor was it emphasized by all the agencies visited. Nevertheless, it was gratifying to find it stressed by many, with good results reported. Insofar as workers are successful in moving toward this aim, the quality of living in large segments of our population will improve, with ample implications for the way these teenagers will bring up their own children. Exclusive concentration on stopping violence is not enough.

## D. School and Jobs

The questions here are whether the workers were able to help keep the youngsters in school, to persuade them to return after they had dropped out, to help them accept training, and find and hold onto suitable jobs. Many examples of success were cited, but they did not approach the numbers of young people to whom these goals are relevant. Influencing factors have been mentioned. Some were within the youngsters, e.g., too long a history of failure in school, too little impulse control, etc. In jobs, as well as schools, the strong feelings against authority often prompted the youngsters to lash out unreasonably. As one boy put it about a job he had left, "too many bosses." Thoughtful workers give careful attention to this authority problem. If the youngster had a "record," job finding tended to be more difficult.

Outside the youngsters' control was the readiness of schools and employers to make allowances for undisciplined behavior, and the capacity of the local economy to absorb young, inexperienced and often untrained employees. In Detroit the workers were most discouraged about job opportunities for youth; in Washington, D.C., the mood was more hopeful. Discrimination was a further obstacle.

Yet, in the face of these problems, many successes were reported, and this set of goals was clearly uppermost in the minds of the workers. Success is influenced but not controlled by the workers. To solve these problems for large numbers calls for far-reaching changes in education and in economic opportunity for youth.

It is fitting to end this chapter with a note of modesty about expectations of change, even with the best work. A staff member of the Chicago Youth Development Project said that he found it helpful to remember something their executive had said: when problems change from very, very bad to very bad, and then to bad, that is progress. A lifetime of experience is behind the behavior and the values of alienated youth and destructive forces continue to operate while the worker tries to stimulate change. Movement is not even; it tends to occur in jerks, with some forward and some backward. It is easier to modify behavior than it is attitudes, although the two are closely inter-related. Change usually does not happen across the board; the old and the new get mixed up together, with strong pulls toward the old. Miracles should not be expected, but healthy changes can be achieved.

## CHAPTER FIVE

WORK WITH ALIENATED youth groups moves in many directions and deals with an enormous diversity of situations and problems. A full treatment of desirable methods could in itself compose a sizable book. Those selected for presentation here have a special importance, but, to keep this chapter proportionate to the rest of

# Methods

the book, their consideration is abbreviated. No attempt will be made to cover the range of methods known to social work and related fields.

## Diagnosis

Basic for intelligently applied and helpful methods is thorough diagnosis, which is the process by which the specific facts are related to relevant theory and values, resulting in the formulation of goals which give purposes and forms to intervention. Without them there can occur the phenomenon of the redoubling of our efforts when we have lost sight of the ends. The diagnosis should include the group, individual members, their families, the neighborhood and any other related factors.

At the very beginning, when a study is made to provide a basis for the decision as to whether service will be offered, care must be exercised in any contacts with the group and others to avoid either an explicit or implied promise of service. Sublower-class people are sadly ready to be disappointed by being let down again by the community.

After service has begun, diagnosis and action interact, each feeding the other. With guidelines from diagnosis, the worker acts, which can also involve being passive. Then the reactions are carefully watched and assessed, with a resulting clarification and re-

formulation of diagnosis. The pattern of interplay between diagnosis and action should continue all through the work with the group.

In some other fields, diagnosis can be done under quieter conditions at a slower pace. However, in streetwork, decisions must often be reached under stress, accompanied by noise, pressure and disorganization, when it is difficult to think at all, let alone to think straight. Regular and competent supervision, thoughtfully prepared and guided staff meetings, and appropriate consultation are essential. Crises among the youngsters are loaded with implications for the future and a superficial or distorted diagnosis can lead to action along one-way and dead-end roads.

A last point about diagnosis is that to varying degrees the teenagers and others related should participate in it. What is called feedback, the reactions of the people served to what the worker does, is one form. More conscious and pointed is the direct discussion of problems with those involved. Some youngsters have remarkably keen insights which can benefit the others through joint thinking, enriched by the worker's support and elaboration. In the long run, helpful as it is for the worker to develop sound diagnoses, the final test is what deepening of understanding the clients themselves carry away into the future. An important dimension of change is the extent to which their diagnoses and those of the professionals converge.

### The Contract or Working Agreement

In several human relations fields the idea is developing that as service begins there should be some clarification of what it involves, mutual expectations, and whether each party wants to enter into the relationship.[1] This approach becomes enmeshed in the suspiciousness of hostile youth groups, their lack of successful experience with verbalizing such matters, and the seeming incongruities to them about the motives of a person and an agency which offer help without an "angle." Nevertheless, some things can and should be done.

The concepts of interest in the young people, concern about

---

[1] For a fuller development of these ideas, see Louise Frey and Marguerite Meyer, *Exploration and Working Agreement in Two Social Work Methods,* mimeographed, available in Boston University Nursing-Social Work Library, 1962.

their welfare, and readiness to be of help in a variety of ways, should be conveyed to them. Offers of assistance with recreational activities and resources may draw the greatest response, but they should be in a larger context of problem-solving so that the worker's role is not perceived as limited to helping them have fun. Nor should the worker present himself as "one of the boys," which would destroy his usefulness. In his eagerness to be accepted and to establish a relationship—until this occurs the worker is in a highly anxiety-inducing situation—there is the temptation to go too far, to over-identify with the youngsters, a criticism heard with some frequency.

Reasonably early, the worker's and agency's commitment to respect for the law should be shared. A balancing point needs to be made clear: the worker is not a stool pigeon for the police and he will be frank with the group about what he thinks it necessary to tell the police. Integrity is his constant bastion.

If the agency and its program are well known in the neighborhood, the worker's task is eased. If not, he faces building his role, expectations and ways of work out of his own efforts, which slows his progress.

Finally, the contract idea is gradual, not completed at the very early stages. New facets will need attention as the relationship deepens. Many eventualities cannot be anticipated, and they must be dealt with as they occur.

### Termination

The termination of service is not always controlled by the agency, as when a large percentage of the group is incarcerated, moves away, enters the armed services or decides against further contact with the agency. When the agency made the decision, it was based on changes in the young people, especially in the decrease or elimination of behavior disturbing to the community.[2] Agencies varied in further criteria, such as deeper attitudinal changes, securing and holding jobs and generally being launched upon the route to productive adulthood. Other claims on the agency's resources were important. A small number of instances were reported of termina-

---

[2] The Crime Prevention Association of Philadelphia has specific and written criteria for termination.

tion because of failure; the agency deciding that it would serve no useful purpose to continue.

A provocative question is whether to have the group members participate in the decision about termination. At first glance, there is a democratic appeal about such involvement, but there are counter-considerations. The group is apt to think in terms of wanting to continue with someone they like who has been the means by which they have had pleasant and constructive experiences. They are apt to see only deprivation in termination. The agency, on the other hand, is conscious of its responsibility to transfer the worker to a group which is more in need of him, and cognizant of the dangers in permanent dependence on the worker. It would therefore seem best for the agency to take responsibility for the decision.

The process of terminating a service which is highly meaningful is not to be taken casually. The preparation should be started well ahead, even months, of the deadline. Careful explanation should be made of the reasons, emphasizing, if true, the gains that the group has achieved, offering an important positive to balance potent negatives. Strong feelings are generated, especially that of being deserted by the worker, and there have been threats that they will act even worse than they used to, thereby trying to show how essential it is to continue the service. It helps to have these feelings come out and for the worker to listen to them with respect, while being calmly firm about the decision to terminate. Opportunities should be provided to recapitulate and evaluate the total experience, with stimulation to think about how learnings from it can be generalized to apply to future situations. The achievement—almost graduation —angle should be stressed, and perhaps even celebrated with a party.

Fortunately most of the agencies left the door open for continued help to individuals after service to the group as a whole was ended. The worker's telephone number was known to the members and he made it clear that he would welcome hearing from them whenever they might need him, a desirable practice. Many examples were cited of such post-termination contacts. Most involved difficulties, but some were related to pleasant occasions, such as promotion on the job and marriage. Even with the most effective work with a group, vulnerability continues to be great, and the life line of the availability of the worker is needed.

### The Relationship

The relationship between the workers and the youth, as well as their families, is a central dynamic for change. It is sometimes mistaken for an ultimate end, which it is not, but it is a wellspring of potentially health-giving waters flowing toward a better future. Its creation requires dedication, patience, skill, a feeling for the teenagers and the harsh realities within which they live, and a sense of fun with the ability to share in their legitimate pleasures. It opens new vistas of trust, activities and community concern and resources.

### A. Stages

The relationship seems to have a fairly typical life cycle, beginning with suspiciousness and much testing on the part of the youngsters. In the language of behavior, they are saying, "We'll show you how bad we are, and then let's see if you still care about us." Occasionally they may take on a honeymoon kind of behavior at the beginning, perhaps fearing to show anything ugly. The worker needs to demonstrate that it is not necessary for them to continue this performance. He communicates the delicate distinction between disapproving certain kinds of behavior and liking and accepting the youth as people, a distinction which fortunately most of them are able to grasp.

It is generally agreed that the leaders must be reached and acceptance won from them before a meaningful relationship with the group can be attained. There are pitfalls in that the real leaders are not always apparent, and the worker may find himself making some false starts. There is also the "gamesmanship" that these youngsters may employ, seeming to be moving out to him but really giving him a snow-job. This is a rough period for the worker, but it is reassuring to know that so many of them have come through it successfully, with relatively few failures.

Then doors begin to be opened, usually by specific occurrences. The worker provides help with interesting activities, trips, a good dance, use of a gym, free tickets for a basketball game, etc. A crisis may arise, such as some of them getting arrested, and the worker joins them in court. Slowly the young people learn that he can be trusted, that he is the key to resources, that he cares about

them, and that he can do practical things for them. Then some of them will turn to him for individual help about jobs, school, family problems, and perhaps, as time goes by, even about drugs, drinking and sex. This is the most productive period of the relationship, but it is not reached at the same time with all, and may never be reached with some.

Finally, there is termination, when hopefully the gains are solidified and preparation is made for next steps, as individuals and as a group, if indicated. With the door left open for further contacts with individuals, the worker has reached the end of the cycle. He began with efforts to create a degree of dependency on him so that there was leverage for change. Then gradually he moved toward the goal of self-sufficiency for the youth, thereby hopefully eliminating the need for his continued attention.

The Youth Development Project in Chicago articulated the stages in this manner:

1) The worker and the group recognize each other.

2) There are contacts; each has some idea of the other and names are known.

3) Association occurs at least once a week.

4) Influence is exerted, the youngsters come to the worker with problems and the families are within his orbit. He is now in a position to exercise some controls.

5) Termination. This stage had not been reached with the groups at the time of the visit.

However the unfolding of the relationship is formulated, its stage of development has important cues for what the worker will do. At the beginning, for example, when the worker is an alien to the teenagers and they need to test him, it would be an error for him to push intimacy by putting his hand on their shoulders or asking personal questions. Action implications grow out of each stage.

## B. Parent-Substitute role

The parent-substitute feature of the relationship has been debated but the writer believes that it is both real and highly significant, especially for youth who often have not had the benefit of sustaining and satisfying parental relationships. One group of girls was reported as putting into words that the group was like a nice

family and the worker like a good mother. Boys are less likely to articulate such feelings, but they do exist and exert force.

Many of these youngsters acutely need the experiences which evolve with a good parent: abiding interest, regularity in living routines, sharing of troubles and joys, and support in times of stress. Most of these the workers contribute when needed, even sometimes to the extent of signing report cards, getting the youngster up in the morning, spending time with him when he is ill, talking with school officials, etc. Here, too, diagnosis is crucial. Many parents in the sublower class take care of these functions well and the worker should not undermine them or invade their prerogatives. However, all too many families are not providing the essential sustenance, emotional or physical, and to their teenagers, the parent-substitute role of the worker takes on strong potential. When the relationship is ripe for it, many youngsters reach out for and make full use of the worker's parent-like functions and activities.

An aspect of the latter which is intangible and elusive is sex identification. Many of the adolescents are confused in this area and a deep-going experience with an adequate and strong adult of the same sex probably contributes to a clearer sense on the part of the adolescent of who and what he is. One mother actually articulated how much she appreciated having a fine male worker in close contact with her fatherless son. With so many fathers absent from the home or inadequate in it, the male worker can be a central source of healthy growth, which can be extended through contacts with other mature and reasonably successful adults. While the girls tend to be somewhat more fortunate with their mothers than the boys are with their fathers, the need is still frequently great for a warm, firm and giving feminine worker.

The predominant practice among the agencies was to assign a worker of the same sex, often of the same nationality or race, as the group. However the Group Guidance Section of the Probation Department in Los Angeles did have some women working with groups of boys. According to the reasoning above, it would seem better to have the worker of the same sex, but there are no clear substantiating data available, and a rationale could be developed to support this agency's practice (it applied to only a small number of workers). The relationships between these boys and their mothers,

and with girls too, are frequently difficult, and women workers can help to create a more mature sense of females. The writer was impressed with the motherly way in which two women at a truce-meeting acted, showing the boys how to use napkins and other things which good mothers often do for their sons. The boys frequently apologized to the workers for their strong language and looked a little uncomfortable when they made derogatory remarks about girls. Whatever may be the best position on this question, the opportunity for the young people to have positive and meaningful contacts with appealing adults of both sexes is a contribution which the worker can make.

It must be recognized that even the most skilled and dedicated workers cannot be fully and completely parents; they do not offer home life to the youth. Therefore, whenever there are potentials on which to build, the real parents should be supported and encouraged to fulfill their responsibilites. When such potentials are absent, a serious gap in community services is faced. Experimentation is needed with foster homes, new kinds of group homes, and camps, which can more fully substitute for the functions of a satisfactory family than is possible for the streetworker. There are enough young people in this almost non-family category to justify major efforts.

## C. Use of Authority

The authority component in the relationship is most challenging to the worker's security and maturity, and it involves his own history. Adults who are still struggling with their own adolescent rebellion against authority usually experience difficulty in exercising it wisely with younger people. Furthermore, the appeal of social work seems to get most response from people who temperamentally feel comfortable with non-authoritative methods and who often find it difficult to set limits firmly and stand by them. And finally, the boundaries between the use of authority justified by and well-rooted in the situation as contrasted with its expression as a need of the worker's personality, are fine indeed. It is all too easy to confuse one with the other.

Except for cases wherein the police, courts and perhaps teachers are the source of the youngsters' contact with the agency, the relationship begins by consent, as it were, with little or no real authority

in the worker and little or no control over the teenagers. Unlike some other community functionaries, he must earn his authority,[3] except for that which may be ascribed to him because of his access to police, courts, schools, employers, and other community resources. To overlook this would turn the worker into a policeman, in the face of the fact that he does not possess the legal base or force which the police have. The strength in the worker's position is his ability to form a trusting and meaningful relationship through which other doors can be opened. If he were to concentrate at the beginning on controlling behavior, he would probably destroy the possibilities of deeper and more abiding changes.

However, when he reaches the stage when he means much to the youth, he should be free to take strong stands about undesirable behavior. In doing so he should demonstrate a mood and method which he hopes will be taken over by the teenagers as a way of living and making decisions. The mood should not be angry nor in the tone of a clash of wills to see who will win. The reasons for his position need to be clear and understandable. Rather than emphasize pleasing him, the stress should be on reality (this theme will be elaborated below), which tends to bounce back and hit the youngsters when they disregard it.

The teenagers have rights as well as responsibilities, and they are often unaware of their rights. Some agencies, such as the Chicago Youth Centers, have built up this point, even to the extent of court action against policemen accused of abusing some youngsters. The latter should be heartened by the demonstration that there can be a steady and just quality to the authority of the law, which entitles them to rights going beyond the caprices of any policeman. There have been encouraging changes in the police in this direction.

In dealing with the gang psycho and his unhealthy personality, the worker may have to be more vigorous and direct in his use of authority. In addition to marshalling the strengths in the others so that they will not follow the psycho, and some blunt talk with him, it may be desirable to call on the police for action as soon as there is a basis for it. Work with the others assumes that a degree of

---

[3] For a strong position on the use of authority, see *Identifying and Controlling Delinquent Groups of Boys* (Ottawa Youth Services Bureau, Ottawa Welfare Council [Ottawa, Canada, 1963]).

rationality is attainable, but with some gang psychos, this state may not be achievable without psychiatric treatment, if then.

The worker's goals in relation to authority are to prevent incidents which are damaging, to help the youth learn to respect reasonable control, and, more important, and long range, to stimulate the young people to internalize authority so that they learn to exercise their own controls. The worker cannot always be with them and there will come a time when he won't be with them at all. Furthermore, continued reliance on the worker to be the conscience, the "no" person, means the prolongation of undesirable aspects of adolescence. Adults need restraint from within.

Recognizing that this latter goal is most difficult to achieve, there are ways into it. Fortunately, the healthier youth have impulses to grow up which respond to meaningful appeals. Crises can be effectively utilized, with great emphasis on the painful consequences of lack of controls. Rewards for restraint are realizable in the forms of community confidence and approval, success in school or job, pride in a well-run dance in contrast to a brawl, satisfying participation in an athletic league, a thoroughly enjoyable trip, and others. The evolution of internally exercised authority in all of us is uneven, but even with highly rebellious youth it can reach a degree of fruition.

## D. "Detached" Relationship

A last point about the relationship involves the adjective sometimes preceding the title of the worker, "detached." It has a somewhat schizophrenic sound, but more seriously it suggests that he is unrelated to the agency. What the term probably means is that he is physically detached from, outside of, an agency building. It would be a distortion and a disservice to the young people to give them the impression that he is not attached to an agency. Throughout, the relationship should be with him as a representative of the agency, which is an integral part of the picture. It is the agency, and through it, the community, which sanction and make possible his work, providing access to the essential resources required for its success. This perhaps obvious point is belabored here because more than the representatives of other types of agencies, this worker operates a great deal by himself out in the neighborhood, in seeming isolation from his agency. There may be the temptation to think in terms of a domain that is his own and a degree of in-

dependence which could chip off parts of his foundation in the agency. Fortunately, many of the workers interviewed seemed to be clear about the agency and community representative features of their functioning.

### Work with Individuals

It was generally agreed that regardless of the character of the group, work with the members as individuals, and with their families, is crucial. Decisions about whom to select for special attention at any given time tend to be made on the basis of the importance of relating to leaders, crises which command attention, and the diagnoses of the various members. There is close and significant interplay between what is done separately with a youngster and what occurs in the group. Other members can be stimulated to reinforce the worker's efforts to help one girl or boy. In one situation, after great effort, a job was found for a boy. One day he asked his friends to tell the boss he was sick so that he could take it easy the next day. Encouraged by the worker, the other boys refused and said that he would be at work even if they had to drag him there.

Access to the individual adolescents is made easier by the group's acceptance of the worker. As a complete stranger offering service to a girl or boy, he would find the going rough indeed. It is not necessary for a well-defined and cohesive group to exist to enable the worker to function with individuals. He needs to be seen, known and accepted in the neighborhood as a helper of young people. The streetworker model is not limited to highly organized gangs. It can function with clusters of loosely related youth.

While the youngsters usually talk big and tough, many of them are deeply lacking in self-confidence and have a poor self-image, accompanied by fears which they try hard to hide. One group of boys was taken on a trip from Philadelphia to Atlantic City, where they sat in the car until the beach was empty, and then went into the water with their clothes on. Many other examples were given of fears of situations which more assured youngsters could take in stride.

The worker has many opportunities for ego building. In Chicago, based in the Sears YMCA, youth talented in singing, dancing, etc. were helped to put on a show in a big hall for a large audience.

This is a dramatic way to give recognition and perhaps pave the way for some of them into a career in the entertainment field. But there are many smaller, yet important, ways of building the sense of self-worth through achievements.

The tangles in the family often have the double impact of giving the youngster the feeling that his parent(s) does not like or respect him and that the family part of his identity is made of shoddy stuff. As the worker interprets each generation to the other and is able to open honest and friendly communication between them, the sense of self and of the family as a whole is apt to improve. Many hours of individual talks with the youth and their parents must be invested with a high order of skill. Some agencies worked with groups of parents whose discussions dealt with the problems of dealing with their adolescent children. Special Services for Groups in Los Angeles has some particularly interesting reports on such parent groups. As parents come to know and trust the worker, they turn to him for help.

Crises are opportunities for assistance with family relationships.

A few girls from one group had run away and their families were upset. The worker offered what comfort she could and asked to be called whenever there was news about the girls. The police picked up the girls about forty miles away, and the worker went with a relative to get them. On the way back, she tried to help the girls understand the implications of this escapade. They were terribly afraid of the reactions of their parents. The worker asked them to stay in the car so that she could talk with the parents alone to soften their anger and prevent beatings. At an appropriate moment she called the girls and stayed long enough to help the families get beyond recrimination and begin to think about how relationships could be improved.

This is but one illustration out of a great many of the strength and opportunities which are generated by having a trusted and resourceful professional on the spot, available when needed. The middle-class pattern of making regular and advance appointments for service is usually not workable for sublower-class families, especially in times of stress.

There are many complexities and subtleties in the individual aspects of this work, both within and outside of the group, but the literature in social work and other fields has helpfully developed

them. Just one further point will be included here—what is said by the youngsters and their families should be listened to with care and respect. Even more important is to search for what they are trying to say and fit it into a diagnosis of the total situation. For example, the youngster cited earlier who strutted around the room shouting how great he was as president of the group and as a ping-pong and pool player, was probably trying unconsciously to say some other things, especially how insecure he felt.

### Reality's Role

The appeals of honesty, justice, sportsmanship and other general moral precepts are not apt to be either new to hostile youth groups or effective. Some leverage is generated by identification with the worker and therefore receptivity to his values. While this is a prized dynamic of change, it is personalized, and the changes must be internalized if they are to have permanent meaning. Reality is a substantial resource which workers can and do utilize, both in prospect and retrospect. When acts are contemplated, the young people are stimulated to examine their probable consequences; when acts have occurred, to point up what can be learned from them. A group of girls, with the help of their worker, had just made satisfactory arrangements for the use of a recreation room in a housing development. On the way out, one of the girls picked up a rock and was about to heave it through a window. The worker pointed out that breaking the window could well result in losing the use of the recreation room. Her appeal to prospective reality was effective; the rock was not thrown. A retrospective example was a group of boys excited about a beating they had given to a member of a rival gang; the worker pointed out that three of their friends were in jail and that they still didn't know what the judge would decide. In this case the appeal to reality was seemingly not accepted by the boys. They argued, which brings up the necessity for referring to reality consequences over and over again. At any given time it may be wise to be brief and not repeat the point if the group is unreceptive, but on other occasions the idea can be stressed again, perhaps with different specific illustrations.

When the mood is excited, calmer and more thoughtful members may not feel free to speak. The worker is likely to know which

youngsters are more reasonable and he can ask them what they think. He can also use specifics such as some of them on probation having just obtained jobs or returned to school, and then ask them to think about what would probably happen if they were arrested again.

If some or all are participating in athletics, he can point out the effects on their physical condition of heavy drinking and drugs. Some agencies scheduled attractive programs at times when the youth tended to have big drinking bouts. Reality can be used with girls and boys about pregnancy and venereal disease. Unfortunately, some neighborhoods and families do not exercise much control over sexual behavior and its consequences, but even here, venereal disease is a threat about which the youth usually have little information. Much can be made of the full meaning of bringing a baby into the world. If there are suspicions that the youngsters are being solicited by drug pushers, the hard facts about being "hooked" and its effects on bodies and lives can be hammered home, perhaps by a doctor.

There is no magic in this reality theme and it sometimes lands on so much emotion and so little rationality that it does not stand a chance, but it is more effective than moral edicts. It has the great advantage of encouraging through immediate and vivid experience a way of dealing with problems, of thinking and living, that builds hopefully for the future. This is sound education.

To guard against oversimplification in the use of the theme of reality, the forces of emotion and irrationality must be recognized. Even the most mature of us, not experiencing the pressures on sublower-class youth, do things which we know will have unfortunate consequences. But the immediacy of painful results can be a powerful argument in many instances. When the hold on reality is genuinely weak, as with some of the gang psychos, psychiatric treatment may have to be pushed. Other group members are helped by the skilled worker to express complicated feelings and attain perspective on them. It is much better for violent feelings to be shared with the worker than to spill out into action. When this does not work, the youngsters need support with their controls, such as calling the police to prevent a rumble.

Some aspects of reality faced by these teenagers are not of their making and are beyond their control, such as racketeering in the

neighborhood, family weaknesses and the lack of suitable and appealing jobs. Changing these is a community and national responsibility. The use of the reality theme applies to what the youth do or might be able to control.

## Utilizing Group Cohesion

Attitudes toward group cohesion varied. Some workers and agencies took the position that strong bonds among members and loyalty to the group are not desirable because such groups are unhealthy. The existence of the cohesion might be recognized as a potent actuality, but the aim was to weaken the group as such to the point of disintegration, while building the individual members and encouraging their participation in healthier groups. The great majority of those interviewed saw good potential in the loyalty to the group and, with certain exceptions, regarded it as an asset. The exceptions included those groups with anti-social attitudes deeply engrained, and entrenched pathological leadership.

This conflict in thinking is more than an intellectual matter; it has vital implications for action. If cohesion is generally desirable, activities should be encouraged which develop the unity of the group. If it is a liability, group activities would be holding actions, with the emphasis mostly on individual contacts facing away from the group. Prognostic judgments are at the base of the issue: one opinion holding that more change is achievable in the members outside of the group context as against the position that work with individuals and the group reinforce each other. Both emphasize attention to individuals; the difference revolves around the group.

When strong cohesion exists, it has meaning to those included, and a worker who sets out to destroy it has a big job cut out for him, and a risky one. By moving too rapidly and directly, he could lose the group. As a responsible professional, he should be reasonably sure of producing satisfying alternatives before trying to take away an important segment of the youth's identity and gratification.

Cohesion, unless it is too far gone pathologically, adds extensions and strength to the worker's intervention. If he is successful in influencing the leaders, the structure of the group carries the flow, like a circulatory system, out to the rest. The same point holds for

success in effecting changes in the group mores. Without cohesion, *all* of the effort must be devoted to individuals one by one, or to only a few at a time. There have been many good experiences building on the youth's concern about their "rep." In the raw state, it tends to be founded on toughness and its facility for producing fear in rivals. The worker, however, with time and skill, can often transform the content of the "rep" into concern about producing a successful and peaceful dance, satisfactory participation in athletics, and other activities which earn new kinds of community approval. With such experiences, group pressures are generated toward non-deviant behavior.

With these changes in "rep," mores and behavior, the residual problems emerge. As the goals of legal behavior, continuing in school and holding jobs, take on living actuality, some members become deviant in a new sense, i.e., they are not able to adjust to the changed standards. They need special individual help, and should not be allowed to block the growth of the others.

Consistent opinion stressed working intensively with one age level in a vertical gang, while making some contacts with and offering help to the other age units, especially the older ones. There was less consistent opinion about the size of the group. There is the potent argument that when a large group exists, even successful efforts to cut it down to a workable number leaves unserved those eliminated. On the other hand, the larger the number among whom the worker's activity is spread, the thinner and more diffuse it becomes. This is a dilemma, but some recourse is available. The concentration can be on the core members, with attention to the peripheral ones only when it is urgent; they may then be freer to find other associations, particularly if fear was a prominent reason for ties with this group. There can also be primary focus on the leaders of a large group, while trying to develop their sense of responsibility for the others.

A careful assessment is in order to judge whether preserving and strengthening the group offer hopeful possibilities. If little cohesion exists, again good judgment is needed for a decision as to whether to try to create it. Putting sick individuals in positions of greater power or promoting the influence of a sick group are dangers to be recognized. Yet there has been a large body of relatively successful experience in working with group cohesion and changing its con-

tent. To a degree, the burden of proof is on the position which
wants to undermine cohesion.

## Group Programming

There is a sizable group work literature devoted to the planning of
group activities [4] and therefore it is important to include here only
matters which are specifically related to alienated youth groups.
Stereotyping of interests and activities and the use of gimmicks,
seemed to be the greatest dangers among those interviewed. Examples are the assumptions that all boys' groups should engage in
sports, even join leagues, that the worker should shake hands with
each member when they meet, and that parliamentary procedure
should be followed. By precipitating groups into these molds, more
problems can be created than solved. The activities should flow out
of the members' interests, readiness and needs, which again call for
diagnoses of the group and the individual members. Furthermore,
unanticipated developments may provide pay dirt opportunities, if
the worker is flexible enough to be ready to take full advantage of
them.

> A group was riding with its worker when a bad accident occurred
> nearby. The boys wanted to go on to their destination, but the
> worker happened to know a good deal about first aid, and he
> stopped and did what he could to help the injured. The boys
> were amazed that he would go to all this trouble for complete
> strangers. This gave him the opportunity to say that he cares about
> people, all people. The conditions probably made an impression
> on the boys which a general speech under ordinary circumstances
> could not equal. Perhaps it helped them grasp his interest in them,
> since they too were strangers to him not long ago.

As suggested earlier, interesting activities can be planned for
times in the week and year when the youngsters are most vulnerable
to difficult incidents. In some instances, it was found that Friday
evenings were occasions for drinking and mayhem. Warm weather
could bring large numbers into the streets at night. Part of the
worker's job is to identify these dangerous periods and to try to fill
them with desirable, appealing activities.

---

[4] For one resource see Gertrude Wilson and Gladys Ryland, *Social Group
Work Practice* (Boston: Houghton Mifflin Co., 1949), Part II, Chapters
VI-X.

Trips are heavily utilized by many of the agencies. Here, too, sound thinking is needed concerning the potential benefits of visiting any particular place, its appeal to the young people, and their readiness to act in accordance with the requirements of the setting. While many of the hostile youth groups are mobile, their orbits are usually highly circumscribed, and trips are ways of opening up new places and people to them. Yet the worker should be sensitive to the impact of such experiences. Driving through attractive neighborhoods may have its benefits, but it can also be depressing. While ready to fight fiercely for the "honor" of their own neighborhoods, many of these groups are ashamed of them and even use derogatory nicknames for them. One was called "Dogpatch," and others questioned why anyone would want to bring up children where they lived. Unless urban renewal offers possibilities for improving the neighborhood for its current residents, or real job opportunities make it possible to move into a better area, seeing elegant homes can well have the effects of reinforcing despair and increasing rebelliousness.

The worker should be alert to the pitfall of being the means for just going somewhere, of driving around and just filling time. His thinking and activities should be purposeful, with goals in mind. Otherwise he can easily be exploited by the unhealthy needs of the youngsters.

Careful preparation of details can make the difference between a successful trip and a miserable one. If the group should have to wait a long time for a program to begin or if it bores them, the result is apt to be trouble, which usually could have been prevented by a few telephone calls and careful thinking. Until such time as the group has firmly established its own controls, the worker should be with them from the time they leave their own neighborhood until they return to it. One inexperienced worker made the mistake of putting a group on its own for the return trip. *A la* the old Wild West they held up the train on which they were riding. A similar point applies to the readiness of the group to use an agency setting when its program is fully under way. Again diagnosis, accurate information about the agency and discussion with its staff as well as the presence of the worker, are all indicated.

Programs should not be limited to recreational activities, although it may be necessary to emphasize them at the beginning.

Problems such as those in school, jobs, relationships with the police, their minority status, sex and other subjects vital to their lives are important possibilities for discussions as the group is ready for them. Accompanying the new surge of experimentation with training, education and supervised work for sublower-class youth, there have been exciting group programs of this nature. It was reassuring to hear from the staff of the Mobilization for Youth in New York that antagonistic leaders and members of gangs worked peacefully side by side, carefully refraining from behavior which might disrupt or destroy the agency's highly valued work and training opportunities. Similar reactions were encountered elsewhere, and they suggest great possibilities for the development of skillfully guided group programs which go well beyond recreational activities.

An important concommitant accomplishment could be the fostering of the youth's ability to verbalize and discuss problems and solutions. They are often impatient with this kind of talk; yet the ability to put such matters clearly, to listen to what others say about them, and to stay with the issues long enough to achieve movement, are essential skills for mature adulthood.

There has been some experimentation with inter-group education. While solid data about results do not seem to be available, this too is worth investigating and trying. It could take the forms of discussions within one ethnic or racial group about their relationships with others, and mixing backgrounds in special programs. In many cities there are Human Relations Commissions and/or Centers at universities whose help could be requested. Many complexities are involved and hasty or casual planning could be disastrous.

A program theme which could be more fully exploited is that of service to others. At a meeting with one of the Chicago Youth Development groups, the boys were folding handbills announcing a movie and speeches for which the admission ticket was one or more cans of food to be sent to Negroes in Mississippi who were cut off relief rolls because they attempted to register to vote. The fact that this was a large-scale effort in which the group was participating added strength to its meaning for them. The boys were quite serious about it.

The program of Youth for Service in San Francisco, as described in an earlier chapter, incorporates another approach. When the

disinherited feel that they are needed by and can do something for others, a new dimension may be added to their sense of themselves.

The possibility of social action, i.e., participating in effecting social change, has been considered but few workable ideas seem to have been developed. It may be that alienated youth groups have been involved constructively in the recent demonstrations. At any rate, the issues should be close and meaningful to youth, and the action needs to be within their abilities and controls. Potential conflict with police is a danger to be avoided if possible. The genes of citizenship may well lodge in social action efforts.

### Truce-Meetings

While far from a panacea, truce-meetings have their uses and are part of the practice of agencies in several of the cities. After a conflict, leadership representatives are called together with their workers, other staff members and sometimes an outstanding person from the community to act as chairman. The group representatives must be strong leaders if they are to be able to carry their gangs along with the decisions reached at the meeting. The timing of the latter is important. If the mood is at a peak of anger and excitement, the session can get out of control and lead to damaging consequences. The meeting-place is usually not announced in advance to the youngsters and each worker brings his own representatives, the point being to prevent large and uninvited numbers from descending upon and disrupting the session. The place should be in neutral territory. Care is exercised to make sure that no weapons are brought along, even to the point of searching the boys, and preparation of the representatives for the occasion is indicated.

The youth may test the newly-declared peace by wandering through the former enemy's area; provocative behavior could easily rekindle the old fires. Active support of the truce with the leaders and other members by the workers is crucial in these inflammatory situations. Just one "blowing off at the mouth" can destroy the laboriously prepared peace.

Truce-meetings have been criticized by police and others for what is perceived as the danger of giving too much prominence and power to gang leaders, or in Yablonsky's context, of dignifying "sociopaths." When group leaders are mentally ill or nearly so, it

would of course be unwise to use the technique. But many of the leaders are relatively healthy psychologically and often have significant abilities which can be directed under guidance toward constructive outcomes. Strengthening their group positions in the context of the peaceful purposes of the truce-meeting can well shift their weight in the direction of more law-abiding behavior.

Another useful practice is that of demonstrating vividly the tremendous impact of rumors on the thoughts, feelings and behavior of the youth. They have the opportunity to try out on each other what they were told or thought they heard. As the rumors get examined and shaken down the worker has a grand opportunity to generalize about the lack of wisdom in acting, even fighting, before trying to find out whether the story is actually true. And how these stories are distorted! A boy had a fight with a member of a rival gang and lost, coming away with bruises which had to be explained. His ego could not stand the truth, so his antagonist became six boys from the rival gang and his friends were, according to the code, obliged to retaliate. So it goes.

The representative character of the truce-meeting carries pressures. Each set of representatives is subject to what has been called an "invisible audience," the rest of the group back home, and those present will want to tell how courageously or even belligerently they spoke for their pals. At the same time, across the table are the others equally motivated in relation to their group. The adults are exerting pressures toward a reasonable mood and the achievement of peace. It is complicated.

One agency tried the technique of making tapes of the truce-meeting and of later playing them to the groups represented. While the results were interesting and debunking, the practice was given up because it put the representatives in the difficult position of having their version of the meeting objectively checked. It tended to stimulate the representatives to concentrate more on saying what later would sound good on the tapes to their friends than on solving the problem at hand.

Truce-meetings can go wrong. History is strewn with unsuccessful efforts to make peace. But, used thoughtfully, skillfully and with sophistication in suitable situations, they are a resource for preventing continued delinquency, injuries and even death.

These thoughts about truce-meetings are impressionistic and

speculative. An important study could be done about them and their consequences. The experiences of individual workers and agencies could well use the rounding out and understanding which can be developed by more investigation.

### Leadership Training

The leaders of groups present key opportunities for influence. There was general agreement among the workers interviewed that these powerful young people must be reached early and late. But there are possibilities beyond the usual ways of working with leaders.

Training could be developed for group leaders to deal with the problems faced by sublower-class youth, demonstrating the various ways in which they could be helpful. Prestige would have to be built into the program, with some compensation for carefully selected leaders. The training should include pre-planned subject matter as well as continuing discussion sessions in which the leaders could present and ask for help with the problems they encounter in fulfilling their responsibilities. Controls would have to be used to make sure that some do not goldbrick, and most of this could be provided through tying them closely to the groups' workers, who should be fully involved at all stages. The Chicago YMCA has a "consultation" plan which resembles in important features the leadership training program suggested here.

Developing regional or national training programs in conference settings, such as many universities have, would add glamor and permit more intensive training. However, it would require for the period of training, the removal of the leaders from their neighborhoods, and would eliminate the simultaneous interaction between the ideas discussed and their application to the groups. It would also nullify the influence of the leaders during the period of the training and create the danger that they would lose their group status. In connection with community development programs in the Far East, it was found that well-trained leaders returning to their villages were sometimes regarded as outsiders no longer in a position of influence. It seems best, therefore, to have the training in or near the city so that the youth leaders can easily move back and forth, and maintain daily contact with their groups.

For the successful operation of this plan, the workers would need to know the groups well, know who the real leaders are and have some ideas as to how both would lend themselves to this approach. Timing could be crucial. If there is violent antagonism between two groups, it might be well to let it cool off for a while before inviting their leaders to participate in the training. Painstaking interpretation of the training program to the leaders and their groups would be essential, with great emphasis on its purpose of helping all of them.

Agencies would have to be committed to the employment of the leaders on a part-time basis, arranged so that the hours would not conflict with school or jobs. The training program could serve as a recruiting base for workers, but this should be a long-range goal, with high school graduation, college and possibly a school of social work in the picture. For probably the great majority of the leaders, this program would not be a career; its scope would be to help them and their groups through the difficult transition from adolescence to adulthood, an added instrument to assist them through the rites of passage.

In effect the leaders would become assistants to the workers, on the spot more and in a strategic position. Their tasks would relate to what is most needed, such as getting a member to a school or job, helping to make arrangements for group activities, trying to cool off hotheads in times of stress, discouraging drinking and drugs, and the like. A sensitive touch would be needed to avoid pushing the leaders toward moving too far too fast to prevent alienation from their groups. The Chicago YMCA puts out a newspaper as part of its "consultation" program. Undoubtedly other ideas would develop with further experience. One possibility is to use these leaders to help with younger groups. They might be in a strong position to influence the younger ones, although some experience suggests that this is not always true. The idea could be tried out on a modest scale. Done thoughtfully, a leadership training program would seem to be a gold mine.

## Community Helpers

Several agencies have found that there are adults in the neighborhoods who are both concerned about the youth and acceptable to

them. It might be a housewife, storekeeper, ex-gang member, or even a bartender. As the worker establishes a relationship with such individuals, he shares with them, respecting confidentiality, his purposes, and enlists their help. If a storm is brewing in the neighborhood, or a youngster is facing a crisis, the aide calls the worker. Chaperones may be needed for a dance and assistance can be used in other ways. To avoid the connotation of spying, the worker should share with the youth what the neighbor is doing and why.

There were some impressive examples of young adults who cared enough about their neighborhoods and their young people to take on such responsibilities as a group and work toward the general improvement of the neighborhood. In one case, with professional help, they succeeded in putting out of business a bar which was having an unfortunate influence on teenagers. More than the specific tasks such adults undertake, their contributions as models, standard-setters and social controls make an impact. It is reassuring to know that so many agencies are working hard to find and develop helpful neighborhood adults. In some instances they serve as assistants to the workers with the groups or as leaders of younger groups for which staff is not available. Care should be exercised in choosing such adults. There was one, self-selected, who regularly made speeches to teenagers about the evils of drinking, while dead drunk himself. With hard work, suitable people can usually be found.

### Role-Playing

Several agencies reported using role-playing; it is a technique which lends itself well to a wide range of situations. If youngsters are worried about a coming interview with an employer, the interview could be role-played before the group, perhaps with the worker taking the part of the employer. The group can then discuss the boy's handling of the situation. If important changes are suggested, the interview can be role-played again. A similar approach could be used to show how a fight starts, how boys interact with police and many others.

A big advantage in role-playing is that it permits living through the handling of a problem without the serious consequences pres-

ent in real life situations. Bad mistakes can be made without having the roof fall in. Additionally it provides perspective and the anticipation and circumvention of pitfalls and pressures which otherwise could catch the youth unprepared.

## CHAPTER SIX

FEW JOBS RELY as heavily on the individual and operate as autonomously as the streetworker's. Some of his most important judgments and actions occur at a considerable physical distance from his agency. Yet he is on the firing line of struggles with many of our society's most difficult and baffling problems. He carries no

# the Streetworker
# and his Career

battery of diagnostic equipment comparable to the doctor's thermometer and stethoscope. He may carry a baseball and other program paraphernalia, but his real equipment is himself, his agency and community resources. Crucial are his motivations, maturity, skills, knowledge and values. They are the blocks on which service is built. And his life is different from most.

### Working Conditions

The unstable and crisis-ridden character of sublower-class neighborhoods deeply affects the kind of life the worker leads. For decades, staff members of settlements, Y's, Jewish Centers and other group service agencies have known what it is to work evenings and week-ends, but the streetworker is subject to the additional strain of not knowing what time of the day or night he will be called to cope with what kind of emergency. It is customary to leave a phone number with the youngsters and sometimes with the families. It may be an answering service (used by many of the agencies), or his own number, or the agency's.

Pressures are great and almost always, there is too much to do with too slim resources. Even supervisors and administrators get caught up in the excitement, the pressures, and the rapid pace. An interview with an executive occurred the day after an inter-gang shooting which hit the headlines. He received numerous calls from the workers and others, and it is to his credit that he was able to give the writer a degree of thoughtful attention. Many on the higher administrative levels regularly go out into the neighborhoods, especially in times of trouble.

All are occupied much of the time by the telephone. The range of contacts described in earlier chapters indicates the need for it. Although appointments with the writer were arranged way in advance, repeatedly they were interrupted by the necessity to answer the phone or to make a call. This is part of the work and it must be accepted.

Some workers placed an understanding wife high among the qualifications for the job. The working conditions make impossible a regular, staid and quiet family life. After the worker returns home from the excitement of settling fights, of taking away weapons, of listening to records or radio at maximum volume, of having been surrounded by incessant and noisy activity, of hours in the ugliest areas of our cities trying to understand what is going on and figuring out what to do about it, he needs considerable time to simmer down, give thought to his own family, and be able to fall asleep.

Yet, in the face of all this, he is not well-paid, and sadly, does not enjoy high professional status, nor is his future clear. It is one of the anomalies of our time that the people who tackle problems so serious, who serve as connecting links between alienated youth and the rest of us, often on lonely outposts, should receive so little recognition and be so minimally remunerated. With their schedules, "moonlighting" would be difficult indeed. The rewards have to be human ones.

With some amusement, one worker told of being stopped by police while walking with his group. They were all searched and the only weapon found was the worker's own pocketknife. Because of the company he kept, it was not easy for him to convince the police that he carried the knife only to sharpen pencils and cut string. The boys were too smart to get caught with knives. Fortunately many agencies have a plan, in cooperation with the police,

whereby the worker carries an identification card. But even with the best planning, he faces suspicion, especially at the early stages, from various sources. Gratitude for his heroic labors is not his daily lot. The satisfactions must be generated out of his feeling for people.

### Motivations and Characteristics

The factual assessment of the complexity of motivations is highly elusive and what follows is based on observations, inferences and what was said by people of extensive experience with street-workers. The desire to help deprived and fenced-in youth stands out clearly and vigorously in many of them. It would be an abuse of psychiatric insight to attempt to claim that these large numbers of workers are primarily motivated by needs to control, to work out problems hanging over from their own youth or by other kinds of underground mechanisms. Purity is rare in these matters, but the primacy of the desire to help is true of the great majority of street-workers, and it was heart-warming to feel its reflection in talking with them.

Many come from backgrounds similar to those of the youngsters. One was described as having spent a term in prison, yet he was said to be constructively effective in his work with youngsters, using the negatives in his own experience to underline what could happen to them. A large number were former gang members who may have used this job as a means for their own upward mobility into professional status. More potent is the point that somehow they came through well. With a "there but for the grace of God" feeling, many wanted to contribute to comparable success for current youth. Some said that conditions were much worse in the neighborhoods where they worked, and they were not sure that they could make it under these greater strains. But the workers rarely gave up. As several put it, there may be hopeless individuals, but there is never a completely hopeless group,—evidence of impressive faith and courage.

Many of the workers had groups of their own race or nationality. Loyalty to one's own kind is often strong and admirable, and it must hurt to see so much behavior which is anti-social and feeds the fires of prejudice. Mature members of minority groups are

caught up in the struggle to break down stereotypes of their wickedness, indolence, lack of honesty, violence, and general inferiority. The workers know that knifings and other acts of violence occur largely because of conditions and causes which rob young people of their self-respect and healthy growth, not because they are Negroes, Mexican-Americans, Puerto Ricans or anything else. Nevertheless, there is apt to be a feeling of urgency about stopping activities which get the youth in trouble, hurt others, and encourage bias.

In this era of large bureaucracies many jobs are hedged about with regulations which prescribe behavior. The streetworker often has something of the maverick in him, and he treasures a high degree of autonomy, which can be a strength as well as a weakness. He enjoys more independence than most. An executive put it by saying that his workers like to possess a "dynasty." The very nature of the job requires relative independence but the too-lone operator can lose the strength and support of his agency and community, and thus destroy his usefulness.

The need for an exciting existence seemed to be strong in many of the workers. A daily routine of regular hours at a desk is not their dish. They are often restless and the job stimulates this feeling. They are subject to the temptation of rushing madly, without giving sufficient thought to what they are doing. Yet, paradoxically, many of them are intellectually alert, read a good deal, and are searching for good ideas. This duality was often present in interviews with them. They responded earnestly, thoughtfully and at length to questions, and yet they would frequently look at their watches and seem impatient about the length of the interview. Many are intellectually hungry and easily get involved in exciting discussions. But sitting still for a long time often seemed to be trying.

Investing so much of himself in the teenagers, the worker runs the risk of taking over their language, and losing part of his own vocabulary and other attributes. He is rooted in two worlds and a balance between them is not easily attained. Much of the identity of the sublower-class teenagers is expressed in their special jargon, varying with the area, and the worker must understand it and be able to use it. Language is a vital aspect of a subculture but there are others, and he must be sophisticated about them. However, he

is deeply rooted in the middle-class world of the community, the agency, his family and higher education, the sources of his strength and his future. He would not only become confused about himself and his responsibilities if he went too far in identifying with his teenagers, but he would puzzle the youngsters. They know that he is different from them and they want and need him to be so.

Self-awareness was frequently mentioned. Some said that they should understand what enabled them to reach healthy adulthood after growing up in vulnerable neighborhoods. As they work in a maelstrom of emotions, their own feelings could easily distort their efforts, especially in relation to such matters as sex and the attitudes of the youth toward the police and the courts. The worker should be free to examine critically his own participation, and high-level supervision is of great help.

There has been much searching discussion about the characteristics of an effective streetworker, but only some of them seem to lend themselves clearly to generalizations. Dedication, abundant energy, a sense of fun, good and quick intelligence, courage, inventiveness, ability to relate to suspicious teenagers, a degree of comfort with authority, and a firm set of values rooted in his own experience, all seem essential. Beyond these, the ice gets thin. Many are athletes with good physiques, yet good jobs have been done by "little guys with glasses." The latter should be familiar with sports but they need not be outstanding performers. Many grew up in lower-class neighborhoods but some with middle-class backgrounds have been successful. Similar diversity applies to the worker's patterns of aggression, his verbal facility and to many other characteristics. There is no standard mold in these matters.

### Educational Qualifications

There was wide difference in the educational backgrounds of the workers. A small number had not finished high school, while some had Masters' degrees, most in social work and fewer in other fields, or were in the midst of graduate study. The great majority had undergraduate degrees. These variations were usually reflected in the level of the responses to the writer's questions, and the interest in tapping knowledge of the thinking and practices in other cities. While education was not the only determinant, there was a

tendency on the part of those who had not gone far in their education to regard their jobs and their agencies as the boundaries of their world, with insufficient curiosity and drive to look beyond for other ideas and ways of work. The orientation of the agency administration was always important, but the influence of the educational background of the worker was far from negligible.

Pages could be filled with delineations of the needed knowledge and skills. Perhaps much of the preceding chapters will suffice to suggest in general what these workers need to know and to be able to do. In addition to the basics of understanding and knowing how to work with people, whether as individuals, groups or communities, there are many other areas which enhance the functioning of the worker. Sooner or later he is apt to find use for practically everything he has learned and to seek new skills. One worker gave his boys haircuts. Questions about venereal disease are apt to arise. Knowledge of the job market is highly useful. It's handy to know where to buy materials for projects. A worker wanted to learn how to make ice cream so that the youngsters could enjoy it and not be tempted to steal for it. One could go on and on.

### Streetworkers as a Subculture

As interviews accumulated with these workers and others who knew them well, general patterns emerged. Characteristic of cultural features, they did not apply to all; they varied with individuals and yet there were striking similarities. There was a strong, almost fierce, dedication to the youth and their problems, with little patience with the society and the community institutions which seem to neglect them. There was almost scorn for what one of them termed the "9 to 5-ers," workers who sit in their offices during regular hours, who don't seem to understand alienated youth and don't reach out to them. This feeling even applied to in-the-building staff members of group service agencies, at times to the streetworkers' own agencies, who were regarded as too middle-class and removed from the arena of spontaneous behavior on the streets. In some instances there was little patience for service to more conforming youth and other segments of the population. There was the general feeling that many agencies were devoting

their resources to needs far less acute than those of sublower-class youth.

In April, 1963, the writer and several workers were leaving the building in Brooklyn in which a branch of the New York City Youth Board was located. They were chatting informally and expressed strong support for the New York Mets, who were faring badly indeed. The implication was clear: "always for the underdog." If subcultures had banners and slogans, "always for the underdog" would set well with the streetworkers.

Less tangible was a sense of not being sufficiently understood or appreciated by the social welfare community, of being somewhat lonely professionally. This was less true of graduates of schools of social work and others identified with social work. The rest were often in a professional no man's land.

When groups of streetworkers are brought together for training, there are tendencies toward impatience with generalized theory and professional lingo, and an eagerness for applications to situations which trouble them. The trainer needs to know their problems, to understand their language, and be ready for their aggression. If he is successful in breaking through, he reaches the dedicated, thoughtful and eager to learn person so many of them are.

### Career Patterns

While most agencies were somehow able to recruit streetworkers, the turn-over was both great and serious. An important factor is that the job is so grueling that its strains can be managed just so long, with advancing years making them harder to accept. Most of the workers were in their twenties and early thirties. In one staff group we were discussing this subject, and there was much kidding of their "old man," who looked to be about thirty-five. The toll on family life is apt to be felt more as the years go by.

The bulk of the jobs are on one level, and the openings above as supervisors and executives are few. The worker who emphasizes planning for the future with the youngsters probably does not overlook his own.

Professional identification takes varied forms. All too many of these workers regard themselves as composing the staff of an agency but not clearly part of a profession. In addition to missing

the stimulation, support and fellowship which being identified with a profession provides, they lose the sense of a life-long commitment, of going somewhere. The present job is transitional. Those trained in and identified with social work have many advantages, not the least of which is the knowledge that reasonably good jobs will be available in many agencies and cities whenever a change is desired.

Added to the career problems of the streetworkers are the low salary and instability of the finances of many agencies. It is small wonder that the turnover is high. Yet, when they leave, what they have learned is lost to the agency—let's hope it is used elsewhere [1] —and the youngsters and their neighborhoods gravely need continuity of personnel.

### Training and Morale

While the curricula of schools of social work do not dovetail perfectly with streetwork, it is the type of professional education that is closest to it. Some agencies are to be congratulated on managing to attract workers with this background, but it does not seem realistic to aim for trained social workers to fill the large number of openings for streetworkers. Some agencies try to fill their supervisory and administrative positions with graduates of schools of social work, a more achievable goal. If larger funds for salaries should become available, and more agencies were able to offer increased professional stimulation, they would be in a stronger position to compete for people with Master's degrees in social work. Only a small number of agencies, mostly voluntary (non-tax supported) ones, are able to do so now.

It is fortunate that most of the agencies insisted on college graduation, but neither a liberal arts education, nor other kinds, with the possible exception of undergraduate social work programs or similar ones such as are offered at Springfield College and George Williams, are designed to prepare students for streetwork. We face the disturbing gap between the need for the highest levels and enormous ranges of skills, and workers who begin with little beyond a

---

[1] It would be interesting to find out what kinds of jobs streetworkers turn to in the years following their agency employment, and whether experiences with the sublower class are utilized and reflected in the later jobs.

general education and perhaps a good life experience. It is tragic to deprive already neglected youth, their families and their neighborhoods of available knowledge and skills. How to fill this need is one of the most troubling questions facing the streetwork agencies, the communities and even the nation. What is being done about it?

Many of the agencies have more or less systematic in-service training programs. As one example, the Chicago Youth Centers had such sessions for an hour and a half every other week. The New York City Youth Board had its own Training Department, but most agencies are not large enough to be able to afford specialized training personnel. Instances were cited of inviting highly competent people to conduct training sessions. Mentioned in an earlier chapter was the plan of United Youth in Cleveland, incorporating monthly training sessions under the guidance of a faculty member of a school of social work, with a psychiatrist sometimes participating. Conferences are utilized. Schools of social work offer special programs relevant to the interests of streetworkers. The training project at Hull House under the auspices of the National Federation of Settlements and Neighborhood Centers, with funds provided by the President's Committee on Juvenile Delinquency and Youth Crime, has had considerable influence, evident in enthusiastic comments made by alumni. It is probable that as university-based training centers financed by the President's Committee develop their programs, more training will be available to streetworkers.

Some agencies encourage their workers to go to schools of social work. The New York City Youth Board had a large number doing so. It was gratifying to find supervisors in some of the agencies moving toward professional training.

Even with this impressive list, the gaps are great, and much more needs to be done. A significant step would be the allotting of stipends by the federal government for streetwork, such as those given to schools of social work by the National Institute of Mental Health for the preparation of outstanding students for practice in psychiatric settings. Experience has demonstrated that these stipends not only attract students but build prestige. Some state funds are available for child welfare and other kinds of social work training. Streetwork should be included, and cities and community funds should move in this direction. Work study plans with schools

of social work could be developed, such as the one offered by the Chicago Youth Centers. With funds available, the agencies could build a plan for training into the contract it makes as it hires workers which would improve both future prospects for the staff member and raise morale.

One significant possibility is to involve the staff in the pioneering venture of developing new knowledge, toward which research is a wide avenue. The next chapter will suggest the conditions necessary to mine what practitioners can contribute to research and how it can stimulate and benefit their services. Another road to pushing back the frontiers of knowledge is good, solid, creative thinking by the staff. It was reassuring to find that some agencies encouraged their workers to write papers; there was a gratifying sense of responsibility for adding ideas to the limited stock available. A third possibility is a conference on a national level of people knowledgeable about streetwork. One was held some years ago and the proceedings [2] were published. Another such conference is being planned.

If these and other steps were taken, added to what agencies are now doing, the streetworker's job would become more attractive, satisfying and stimulating. Increased funds should make it possible to decrease the worker's load and allow him more time to recuperate from the pressures of his job. The attempt should be made to have a wide salary range for the worker's level so that he could look forward to substantial increments. At present, the need for more income often forces him to leave the job, frequently during the period when he is most competent and productive. Salary increases to higher levels would counteract this factor. With these developments, his morale and status would rise, as would the prestige of this type of work, and turn-over would probably decrease. As he reaches the age when streetwork becomes too rigorous, he would be qualified for other jobs.

### Training Needs

The workers' responses to questions about their training needs showed surprising consistency. Frequently the first area empha-

[2] Mary E. Blake, *Youth Groups in Conflict* (Children's Bureau [Washington, D. C., 1958]).

sized was that of increased skills in working with and understanding individual and family dynamics, as well as psychopathology. This was even true of staff members of agencies which emphasized the sociological and belittled the importance of psychology and psychiatry. Apparently at this point the impact of the workers' daily experience was greater than that of the orientation of the agency.

A second common theme was group work with the desire for further knowledge and skill. A third was the interaction between social welfare institutions and the community. Interest was expressed in learning more about subcultures. Great emphasis was placed on developing better diagnostic skills. (These areas make up a large part of the curriculum in graduate schools of social work.) Other concerns were more miscellaneous, such as coaching athletics, methods of securing jobs for the young people, and public relations.

## CHAPTER SEVEN

**Perspectives**

Research is riding high. At times it attracts money for service programs which could not otherwise be obtained. Whenever a puzzling problem is encountered by practitioners, the temptation is to request research. The status of researchers (and probably the salaries), whether social scientists or social workers, is high.

# research

This development among streetwork agencies is both healthy and hazardous. It has already produced valuable findings, with more to come, but it has created tensions and unwelcome burdens. The human tendencies to operate in terms of good or bad and indulge in fads need watching in relation to research as well as in other matters.

The orientation of this chapter is to the actual and potential contribution of research to the more effective solution of the problems of alienated youth, its vast implications for strengthening and sharpening the practices of the agencies which serve them and for new approaches. Other types of investigation may legitimately aim for new knowledge regardless of its usefulness. Research has the great advantages of stimulating a fresh look, often forcing new perspectives. The streetwork agencies, like others, are subject to "institutionitis," to coin a word. The social scientists who do the research are often concerned about improving service and solving human problems. But they have a potent reference group in the community of their fellow social scientists where the values (and the stairway upward) are truth building, theory formulation and good research design and execution. All three can be of great benefit to the practitioner but there can be and have been troubling conflicts. Some result from the bringing together of two or more

professions and the adjustments that each must make to the orientation of the other. A degree of conflict is innate and should be recognized as such. It can be a healthy association if there is mutual understanding and respect which avoids the top dog-lower dog mood. Each has emphases, pressures and goals not shared completely by the other. The tensions between them can lead to growth on both sides. Unfortunately, it has not always been so.[1]

The question of the degree of certainty to be attached to research findings is complex. The assumption that a study done within the rigors of social science requirements results in more exact truth than that uncovered in the practical experiences of thoughtful people on the firing line of service is often, but not always, valid.[2] As researchers usually recognize clearly, there are many traps. The basic assumptions or theoretical commitments of the researcher affect the instruments he devises, and create channels for collecting and organizing data which tend to exclude those not relevant to his intellectual framework. An illustration: if he is primarily oriented to the origins of delinquency in the youngster's early family history within the framework of psychoanalysis, he is not apt to have antennae to pick up waves emanating from cultural or blocked socioeconomic origins. Raw data take on meaning only if they are organized into or lead to theory.

A most perplexing research problem entailed in dealing with groups of anti-social youth is the plethora of variables to be considered: individual and family dynamics; the structure, relationships and values of the group; the impact of other groups; the character of the neighborhood; social class; economic conditions; services to the area; the quality and the approach of the streetwork agency and its workers; and many others. If only some are in focus, how will it be known that they are the crucial variables and that those omitted had no impact? If the attempt is made to include all variables, the researchers may suffer the fate of the juggler with too many balls in the air. No matter how carefully it is done, there

[1] For recognition of this problem and a plan for dealing with it, see Hans W. Mattick and Nathan S. Caplan, *Chicago Youth Development Project: Street Work, Community Organization, and Research,* April 1, 1962, pp. 74 and 75.
[2] For a helpful and balanced presentation of the complexities and potentialities of evaluation research, see Elizabeth Herzog, *Some Guidelines for Evaluative Research* (Children's Bureau [1959]).

is always the possibility that the unmatched characteristics are the most significant in relation to differences between developments in the experimental (given the service) and the control groups (not served or served differently). The Chicago Youth Development Project and the Youth Studies Center at the University of Southern California are working on matching neighborhoods, and have gone to great lengths to find control areas as nearly similar as possible to the experimental ones. This approach seems to have good potential but it is subject to at least two recognized limitations. For one, changes not caused by or specifically related to the service can occur unequally and differently in the two areas. Illustrations are population movement, urban renewal, the construction of an expressway, economic developments, and new schools. The researcher holds his breath in the hope that they will not muddy the purity of his controls. A further problem is that the activities of the workers are not easy to contain within the experimental area. Members of their groups moving from one section to the other, might have relationships, friendly or hostile, with youth in the control area. The workers, dedicated to the youth, do not easily give up on the crossing of lines because it confuses the research.

Another limitation faced by research is the character and quality of the service program it is testing. If the agency does not use psychiatric consultation, and some do not, the study cannot reflect the effects that such consultation might have. If the workers are untrained and the agency is making little or no effort to put them in touch with available knowledge and skills, the research is cast in this mold and cannot reflect a stronger service. If, as was true of the Special Youth Program in Roxbury (Boston), the whole program was confined to three years, including the initial stages all the way to termination, a change in the executive along the way, and service to groups varying from ten to thirty-four months, significant consequences are involved. Time—a generous amount of it—is an essential ingredient in effecting changes in the mountainous pathology which exists in alienated youth groups and their environs.

The extent to which each group and neighborhood is typical of others is difficult to determine. Only as studies increase can we develop security in generalizations. The writer's interviews suggest

that there are common patterns, but that differences among groups and neighborhoods are significant.

In some instances research was being done more or less from the inside, with the researchers hired by the agency. Others were administered from outside the agency's structure. The inside type has the potential—not always realized—advantage of being closer to the service and less in conflict with it, but also the danger of being more biased in favor of the agency. Research administered from the outside is subject to the same factors reversed, i.e., greater distance from the service and less emotional involvement in its activities.

The point of the preceding discussion is to place research into perspective, not belittle or undermine it. The uncritical acceptance of its findings can lead to distorted planning of services and the placing of too much responsibility on the researchers. A particularly regrettable position into which a few research programs have been pushed, or may have sought, is that of judge and jury passing a life or death sentence on the service agency. Evaluation research is now the vogue, and foundations and government bureaus have made grants on condition that the programs thus supported come up with concrete findings. Superficially, this wedding looks felicitous but it runs the danger of diseased issue.

When the researchers' findings will decide the fate of the agency, how must the workers feel about providing them with data which could result in the elimination of their jobs? Can they function at their best under these conditions? How must the researchers feel about playing God? Is this the way to objective and calm evaluation?

It would be quite different if they were charged with deriving maximum learning from the service program, but to provide the essential base for a decision as to whether it should continue may overload research with a responsibility for which it is often not ready, disregard the complexities presented in this chapter and create tensions in the workers. Agencies need evaluation, but it should be undertaken with care, sophistication, and humility.

It is relatively rare to hear of research which has the job of determining whether a child guidance clinic, the Boy Scouts, a family agency or many others should *in toto* continue. Research in such settings is more apt to be addressed to specific problems or pro-

gram features, aiming at increasing the understanding and effectiveness of practice. Yet newer delinquency services, especially streetwork, tend to be put in the defensive position of justifying their existence. Whether this is because they share with Public Assistance and Aid to Dependent Children service to those who are at the bottom of our society and therefore weak politically and otherwise, or for other reasons, is hard to fathom. It is extremely dubious that an objective basis exists for the assumption that these streetwork agencies are needed less and achieve less than agencies whose very survival does not depend on the findings of a study.

Excellent minds are investigating alienated youth groups and impressive findings are already available. As these accumulate and are fed into practice and tested by it, guidelines will develop and policy and planning will become more enlightened.

This chapter would be disproportionately long if it attempted to include all the known research projects. Only brief illustrations can be offered and presented according to categories of subject matter.

### Alienated Youth Groups, Their Families and Neighborhoods

Our understanding of such youth has been considerably advanced by a range of studies. For the sake of economy of space, older ones, such as Thrasher's [3] classic study, will be omitted. Miller, using material from the Special Youth Program in Roxbury (Boston), has written extensively on the cultural characteristics of the sublower class, and has developed and elaborated on aspects such as their special patterns of adolescence, the matriarchal family, delinquency, sexual behavior and others. While there has been much controversy about Miller's theoretical positions, his work has the somewhat unusual strength which derives from a blending of a mass of data painstakingly organized with articulated theory. Samples of his writings are included in footnotes [4], [5] and [6]. Two

[3] Frederick M. Thrasher, *The Gang* (Chicago: University of Chicago Press, 1927). It is to be reissued soon with an introduction by James F. Short, Jr.
[4] William C. Kvaraceus, Walter B. Miller *et al.*, *Delinquent Behavior* (National Education Association [Washington, D. C., 1959]).
[5] Walter B. Miller, "City Gangs: A Report on the Mid-city Delinquency Study," *Boston University School of Social Work Journal*, I, (January, 1963).
[6] Walter B. Miller, "Lower Class Culture as a Generating Milieu of Gang Delinquency," *Journal of Social Issues*, XIV, No. 3, (1958).

summary volumes are to be published: *City Gangs: Cultural Milieu, Customary Behavior and Delinquency* and *City Gangs: An Experiment in Changing Gang Behavior*.

Kobrin, at the Institute for Juvenile Research in Chicago, has long been engaged in delinquency research, with interest in its group aspects. At the time of the writer's visit, he was studying what becomes of youngsters when they reach the later twenties, a much-needed approach strengthened by a good deal of knowledge of these same youth during their adolescent years. Follow-up studies in this field have been far too few. An informal study was described of the ebb and flow of delinquent activity in relation to group solidarity, and types of leadership. Other studies dealt with the proportion of boys participating in gangs (fifty percent in one area), and with the relation between "character structure" delinquents and the social position of the family in the neighborhood. An interesting hypothesis was that gang leaders came from families just below the elite.

Reference was made in Chapter II to Spergel's work [7, 8] in developing the categories of racket, conflict, theft and drug gangs, and of relating each to the socio-economic factors in the neighborhoods.

Mobilization for Youth in New York is doing extensive studies [9] of individual and group behavior and characteristics. Material had been developed about the area and many facets of the behavior of its population. With Mobilization's varied, extensive and imaginative program, later research should yield impressive results.

The work of the Youth Studies Center of the University of Southern California seems to be concerned mainly with an assessment of the relative effectiveness of more intensive services in an experimental area with that of less intensive services in control areas; [10] the methods used should yield much important information about

---

[7] *Op. cit.*

[8] Irving Spergel, *Exploring Delinquent Subcultures* (mimeographed, undated).

[9] For a prospectus of research plans, see *A Proposal for the Prevention and Control of Delinquency by Expanding Opportunities* (New York: Mobilization for Youth, Inc., August, 1962), Chapter V and the Research Appendices.

[10] *Progress Report, Study of Delinquent Gangs* (Los Angeles County Probation Department and Youth Studies Center, University of Southern California [July 1, 1961—June 30, 1962]).

the gangs and their members. Additionally, the Youth Studies Center made an application for funds March 1, 1963, to the National Institute of Health entitled "The Nature and Roles of Female Delinquent Gangs." The target groups of girls are related to the boys' groups already under study. As indicated earlier, our knowledge of girls' anti-social groups is much more limited than that of boys', and this proposed study could help fill the gap.

A large research program was developed at the Chicago YMCA. While much of it is in the early stages, some articles have been completed.[11]

Meriting attention are publications not based on formal research, but which draw on extensive experience thoughtfully interpreted. The previously mentioned *Breaking Through Barriers* from the Welfare Council in Chicago, various publications of the New York City Youth Board, and *Proceedings: Institute on Work with Youth in Conflict,* University of Illinois Division of University Extension, June 15-17, 1959,[12] are illustrations.

### Prediction

The wherewithal to foretell which children are likely to become delinquent would help considerably in prevention. Using a modification of the well-known prediction scale formulated by the Gluecks, the New York City Youth Board studied all boys entering a school and is following them to the age of seventeen, to determine whether the prediction about each was fulfilled. The focus is upon individuals but if the prediction scale is substantiated, it will have important implications for groups and the distribution of services.

Since the scale is based on family relationships, sooner or later the influences of peer culture, the neighborhood, the opportunity picture and other factors should be considered.

### Evaluation Research

This is both the most demanded and complicated category. The findings travel fast; they may have great influence on decisions

11 For example, James F. Short, Jr. and Fred L. Strodbeck, *The Response of Gang Leaders to Status Threats: An Observation on Group Process and Delinquent Behavior,* revision of a paper read at the annual meeting of the American Sociological Association, August, 1961, mimeographed.

12 Included in the *Proceedings* are presentations by Solomon Kobrin and Saul Bernstein.

about granting funds in many cities in addition to the one in which
the work is done. The Chicago Youth Development Project [13] in
cooperation with the Institute of Social Research, University of
Michigan, carefully prepared an evaluation design as it was planning its service program. It is using control areas matched with the
experimental ones. At first the two were contiguous, but it was
found that better matches were in some dispersed areas, i.e., some
controls were adjacent to the areas served by the agency and others
were not. Problems about control areas mentioned earlier in this
chapter were recognized.

In addition to obtaining police, court and detention data, the
Youth Development Project plans to have interviews with the boys,
their parents and key neighborhood people about attitudinal
changes. Furthermore, the judgments of the staff will be secured.
Special attention will be given to crucial situations and how workers responded to them, with emphasis on the sequences of events
which led to success. The relation between characteristics of the
workers and success will be studied.[14]

Miller's article [15] calls for somewhat detailed consideration. He
describes the Special Youth Program in "Midcity," stating its rationale and such facts as the dates of the operation, June, 1954, to
May, 1957, and that seven workers (five men and two women)
served about 400 youngsters in twenty-one groups. Of the latter,
205 members of seven groups were given intensive attention. Miller
used three criteria for testing the effectiveness of the agency: 1)
disapproved forms of customary behavior; 2) illegal behavior;
3) rates of court appearances.[16] (It is noteworthy that Miller
found reports written by the workers to be fuller sources of information than were official records, a point also mentioned elsewhere. It supports the writer's reliance on workers' statements.)
In all three categories, Miller found that the decreases were so

---

13 *Ibid.*

14 For the approaches used by this agency, see the first footnote of this
chapter, and Nathan S. Caplan, *et al, The Nature, Variety and Patterning
of Street Club Work,* presented at the meetings sponsored by the Youth
Studies Center of the University of Southern California, Los Angeles,
August 26, 1963.

15 Walter B. Miller, "The Impact of a 'Total-Community' Delinquency
Control Project," *Social Problems,* X, No. 2 (Fall, 1962).

16 *Ibid.,* p. 177.

slight as to be "negligible." He allows for various other kinds of achievement, but clearly claims that very little was accomplished in the direction of decreasing disapproved-of or illegal bahavior.

There are many questions.[17] As Miller makes clear toward the end of the article (page 190), his findings are at the "most gross analytical level," i.e., they do not really take account of the differences among the groups, variations in behavior patterns, and certain changes over time referring to the variations in the duration of work with the groups. One amounted to only ten months.

Of the seven groups, Miller indicates that the two composed of girls did not follow the pattern of negligible change away from violative behavior. In some respects, a group of younger, white and not so lower-class boys are presented as less negative. This leaves four groups in the failure bin. One group, served by this agency and studied in a thesis,[18] was described as highly pathological, perhaps raising a question as to whether they should have been worked with as a group. The writer does not know whether Miller's seven groups included this one. If they did, the "gross" results must have been seriously affected.

Also the article does not go into the relation between the length of time devoted to the group and the changes which occurred. It is not reasonable to expect significant and lasting developments much before two years, judging by what workers in various cities said. Some of the groups Miller studied were given service for more than two years, and some less, but he does not go into the connection between duration of service and results.

Miller makes the constructive point that the most clearly lower-class groups, i.e., the furthest from community standards, are apt to produce the greatest obstacles to change. In all fields this tends

---

17 Tangential but significant is the way Miller presents the training of the workers and the methods they employed. He uses such terms as "psychodynamic psychotherapy," "group dynamics" (which has several meanings, not all of which apply), "group therapy," "sociocultural and psychological concepts and methods." He does say that the workers were "competent and professionally trained," but neglects to mention that the core of what they were doing was group work with a general social work orientation. The terms quoted above are related but they do not describe the methodology, and group therapy is clearly what they were not trained in.

18 Martin Margulies, "Measuring Changes in the Behavior and Attitudes of Street Corner Groups towards an Agency with a Detached Worker Service" (Master's thesis, Boston University School of Social Work, 1959).

to be true. Medicine experiences the greatest difficulty with diseases most advanced, psychiatry with the most psychotic, and so on. How much the most anti-social groups contributed to the end product is not elaborated.

In presenting the methodology of the workers, Miller takes account of termination; yet, in comparing the behavior of the youngsters in the first and last thirds of the workers' attention, this impact is lost.

In assessing the court appearances of the youngsters served by the Project, Miller used control groups matched as nearly with them as possible. In addition to the cautions indicated before on the feasibility of matching control and experimental groups in all significant respects, it is noteworthy that the evaluation research in Chicago and Los Angeles described above, both starting some years later than Miller's, did not use control groups. Furthermore, a staff member of another agency who knew one pair of groups said that he would expect more delinquent activity from the served than the unserved; that if in this instance the project was able to decrease delinquency in its group to the level of the control's, it was an achievement.

Miller presents two tables delineating the court appearances of Project and control group members. One indicates five Project groups and the other four. Why, out of seven groups intensively served and studied, only five were included in one table and four in the other, is not explained. If it was because the excluded groups had no or few court appearances, this would be highly significant, meriting comment.

In 1959, Miller wrote an article [19] covering some of the same territory. In this case he divided the workers' spans of attention to the groups into quarters, rather than thirds, as in the 1962 paper. The reason for the change is not explained. In the 1959 paper, he makes the point that the findings were tentative, but reported that law-violating acts had been substantially reduced [20] to the extent of a net decline of twenty-five percent, and he related this achievement to the efforts of the workers. Considering that the

---

[19] Walter B. Miller, "Preventive Work with Street Corner Groups," *The Annals* (American Academy of Political and Social Sciences [Philadelphia, March, 1959]).
[20] *Ibid.*, p. 101.

target area was selected by the agency because of its unusually acute problems, the reported accomplishments are impressive. Additionally, Miller added that commitments to correctional institutions decreased, age units in vertical gangs became more separated, best results were attained through greater contact with the groups, and changes not directly involving delinquency seemed to be related to the individual worker's focus, e.g., one gave a lot of attention to the negative attitudes in his group toward the police, with good results. In the 1959 article Miller takes account of the reactions to the news that the program was to be terminated, and of the provocative behavior by groups outside its area. At the end he speculates that its "true potential" was not fully realized because of the three-year span and other limitations. It should be kept in mind that both articles dealt with the same youngsters and the same program.

Anyone considering starting a streetwork program, or granting funds to one, would be highly encouraged by the 1959 article, published two years after the experiment ended, and about four years after the beginning of Miller's research. Certainly it could not be accused of being hasty. Yet three years later, in 1962, the achievements in relation to delinquency become "negligible." In the later article, Miller explains the discrepancy in terms of new data, the introduction of control groups, etc., but these would seem to be partial and unsatisfactory. The readiness to change conclusions with shifts in data is admirable, but is it wise to submit the reading public to the risks involved? If this was done by a person of Miller's recognized competence, where is it apt to lead in less-skilled hands?

While there is a paucity of other evaluation studies, a few are available. In an article [21] presenting the Hyde Park Youth Project in Chicago, John M. Gandy indicates that forty-six percent of those studied showed a reduction in anti-social behavior. With twenty-two percent showing no anti-social activities at the beginning or end, the percentage of change among the more deviant was even more significant. This Project did not entail as intensive research as did the Special Youth Program, nor are the categories exactly

---

[21] John M. Gandy, "Preventive Work with Street Corner Groups: The Hyde Park Youth Project, Chicago," *The Annals* (American Academy of Political and Social Sciences [Philadelphia, March, 1959]).

comparable to Miller's, but the findings on streetwork are more hopeful.

There was a somewhat different focus in a study performed by the Neighborhood Youth Association in Los Angeles.[22] The aim was to test the effectiveness of adding casework to group work services, but the findings are of more general interest. Two groups were given both types of service, and two had only group work. The four groups included thirty individuals, and the experiment ran from 1957 to 1959. The follow-up study found that only four of the thirty were delinquent [23] about three years after the end of the experiment, whereas the earlier use of the Glueck prediction scale would lead to the expectation of a much larger number of delinquents. There was improvement in other important respects, such as learning how to deal with problems and the performance of siblings in school. Surprisingly, there were not significant differences between the groups which had casework and group work, and those which had only group work, although there were cases of families which seemed to benefit substantially from casework help. It is significant that the interviewees talked with pleasure about their group experiences and gave them credit for important changes in their lives. A few said that their neighborhoods were so bad that they had to stay home during leisure hours to keep out of trouble. The point was made, in agreement with Miller and others, that it is more difficult to help youngsters from the worst neighborhoods.

A pamphlet [24] published by the Ottawa Youth Services Bureau was based on material from the Huntington-Gifford Hard-to-Reach Youth Project in Syracuse, New York, and from a somewhat similar program in Ottawa. Seven groups were studied from various points of view, including that of "police complaints and arrests," comparing the histories of the youngsters prior to streetwork service with the picture varying from ten months of service, to after fourteen months of service and after eighteen months following termination. The results do not easily lend themselves to statistical

---

[22] *Changing the Behavior of Hostile Delinquency Prone Adolescents* (Neighborhood Youth Association [Los Angeles, 1960]). Follow-up study, 1962.
[23] *Ibid.*, p. 17.
[24] *Op. cit.*

summary, but the decrease in "police complaints and arrests" is striking—more impressive than were improvements in school performance.

### Methods

This area, to which relatively little research has been devoted, needs it as much as, if not more than, others. An impressive stock of wisdom has been accumulated by thoughtful practitioners sensitive to the reactions of the youngsters and others to the methods employed. It needs to be tested, however, to the extent feasible, by more rigorous research methods. The latter are apt to precipitate us into the complexities of evaluation, because methods are good or bad in terms of the results they achieve. What has not been sufficiently tried in research on methods of work with hostile youth groups—nor in some other human relations fields—is a less global, more modest approach. The tendency has been to look at results *in toto,* and then it is difficult, if not impossible, to know what the impact is of any specific method. If one or a few of the techniques were selected, and a large number of incidents involving them collected, their effects, short and long-range, would then be available for study. Those that could be investigated include the firm use of authority, group trips, the building of new leaders to counteract the influence of unhealthy ones, discussion of intergroup relations, and truce-meetings. To offset the fragmented character of incidents, a broader diagnosis of each situation could be included.

There are elements of this suggestion in Miller's research in that he has given some attention to the changes in the youth in relation to the worker's focus. The Chicago Youth Development Project's interest in crucial incidents and what the worker does about them is relevant, and this agency produced an interesting paper [25] illustrating how a worker's seemingly fruitless efforts with a difficult boy are observed by other group members and tend to have a surprising impact on them. The activities of the worker are being studied by the Youth Studies Center at the University of Southern California. They may throw much needed light on the methods which

---

[25] Hans W. Mattick and Nathan S. Caplan, *Stake Animals, Loud Talking and Leadership in Do-Nothing and Do-Something Situations,* presented at meetings sponsored by the Youth Studies Center of the University of Southern California, August 25, 1963.

are or are not effective. In each of these instances, however, the
emphasis on method is somewhat incidental to the other investigation goals. Studies are genuinely needed wherein method is the
primary target.

### Services in Relation to Community Problems

There have been many studies (often called surveys) of agencies,
at times of all those in a community, at others of a segment of
them, and at still others of a single agency. Usually the problems
with which they are working are examined in the context of their
programs. There do not seem to be many such surveys of streetwork agencies specifically, but a few merit attention.

In Los Angeles, Pinamonti, in cooperation with a Study Committee and under the aegis of the Metropolitan Recreation and
Youth Services Council, made a study [26] of Special Services for
Groups, Neighborhood Youth Association, and the Group Guidance Section of the Probation Department, with some attention to
other agencies. Information about the aims, programs and financing of these agencies is included. More inclusive content is found
in the "Summary of Findings." [27] For example, twenty-six workers
served 221 groups, but the need for service was much greater, especially for Negro youth; Los Angeles was spending less than a
third as much as the New York City Youth Board for streetwork;
and reduced work loads and better-trained staff increase effectiveness. The costs per individual served ranged from an estimated
$200 annually for the Group Guidance Section, to $600 for
Neighborhood Youth Association, with Special Services for Groups
in between.

A somewhat different kind of study [28] was made in Philadelphia,
apparently sparked by a question raised by the Community Chest
on the "propriety of settlements engaging special staff to work with
gangs," with the possibility of overlapping the work of the Crime

---

[26] Guido Pinamonti, *Special Social Group Work Services: A Study of the
Role Which Voluntary Community Chest Funds Have in Support of this
Service in the Los Angeles Area* (Metropolitan Recreation and Youth Services Council [Los Angeles, October, 1962]).
[27] *Ibid.*, p. 50.
[28] Area Youth Work Committee, Health and Welfare Council (Philadelphia, July, 1960, mimeographed).

Prevention Association. The Area Youth Committee defined its charge more broadly and critically examined this type of service and the need for it.

A distinction was made between "Street Club Work" (with more seriously deviant groups) and "Neighborhood Youth Work" (with the less deviant who may be potentially serious problems). Characteristics of the groups and the roles and functions of the workers were presented. The ratio of one worker for each more deviant group was recommended. (The majority of the agencies visited by the writer could not afford this, although they probably would have found it highly desirable.) A worker was thought to be able to handle three to five less-disturbed groups.

Statistics about the number of workers and groups served were included. Through various sources, information was assembled to the effect that seventeen additional identified groups needed intensive service, with three more highly probable, calling for twenty more workers; it was estimated that twenty-eight new workers were needed to deal with less-deviant groups identified as in need of service. At a conservative estimate, with relatively low salaries, these added services would cost about $300,000 (probably per year).

The Committee recognized the difficulty of raising this sum but urged that government units, the United Fund and foundations should try to supply it. Other recommendations were made, and the report was specifically geared to state the needs and secure appropriate action.

### Suggestions

The examples of research described above are not meant to be inclusive, but they do illustrate the range of approaches and subject matter. At various points in this book, problems requiring research and demonstration attention were identified, such as illegitimacy, the use of alcohol and drugs, and the residual problem. The most productive approach to them would probably be a combination of experimentation with research, i.e., to try out carefully formulated methods and to study rigorously their effects. It should be done on a large scale sufficient to cancel out the special features of specific groups, neighborhoods, cities and workers, so as to make general-

ization valid. Tackling one problem at a time, and dealing with it in depth and breadth, may prove more productive than studying simultaneously the great range of problems these agencies try to solve.

The meshing of research with practice is a delicate operation, with the polar dangers that the workers might not be ready to adapt to the requirements of research and the extra work involved, or that the researchers could be so preoccupied with the purity of their design that the agency's services could be strained. Workers should be more than sources of information, and should be encouraged to participate appropriately in decisions about research. While they are usually not expert in investigatory method, they know their clients well, and may have good ideas as to what will be acceptable to them in terms of interviews and the like. They are apt also to be aware of the problems needing study. Without participation of these and other kinds, the worker would tend to feel like a lackey, with unfortunate attitudes toward the research to be expected. If he regards the study as vitally devoted to the development of knowledge he can use, ideas he can test in his practice, he will look upon the researcher as a partner in an exciting and important enterprise. Some studies might well be done independently by social scientists, but if practitioners are involved, they should be dignified as partners.[29]

Research can too easily be regarded as the source of all answers. It does have the excellent attributes of forcing people to think, making explicit their assumptions, theories, criteria and methods. But workers are daily trying out ideas and observing reactions to them, thereby deriving much wisdom. Research should not be the only road to good, hard thinking and the search for new ideas. It is slow-moving, expensive, can cover effectively only a limited territory, and the amount of it available cannot begin to deal with all the questions pushing the practitioner for answers. He must use his own resources productively.

A final thought is that there needs to be a balance between research and service. When funds are inadequate and many groups are neglected, as seems to be true practically everywhere, it is a

---

[29] For an interesting example of a mutually enriching relationship between research and practice see Ralph Kolodny, "Research Planning and Group Work Practice," *Mental Hygiene*, XXXXII, No. 1, (January, 1958).

serious step to devote large amounts of money to research. But this can be and has been the justification for financing so little research that the services lose the potential benefits of the new knowledge that through studies might have developed. As a counterpoint, there is the responsibility for being certain that the issues studied are pivotal and will be handled on a high level. Furthermore, research usually does not provide short cuts. At some point, and right now would be best, much larger sums will have to be devoted to service of alienated youth. Research can contribute much, but it is not and cannot be a substitute for increased services.

## CHAPTER EIGHT

THE AMERICAN DREAM is spun out of the vital fibers of opportunity. What one's background is, whence and from whom he came, should not matter. What he is, can do and can become, are the stuff of which our democratic aspirations are made, with the assumption that the upward escalator is running for those with the will, energy and ability to get on.

# the Opportunity

# Problem

But massive blockage has developed, as described in Chapter One. Minorities in our cities in the past managed, in large numbers, to move up, but today hopes for their counterparts are sadly dimmer, economically, socially and culturally. The existence of this obstruction has been acknowledged as one of the most valid causations of sublower-class delinquency. Some regard it as *the* one cause.

The people interviewed, all in one way or another steeped in work with delinquents, agreed that blocked opportunity is a basic component of the entire problem. There were differences as to whether it is the only cause and some questioning of its primacy, but none regarded it as negligible or far down on the list. Many instances were cited of thefts of what the youngsters very much wanted and could not afford, and of the subsequent cessation of this and other kinds of delinquency when a satisfactory job was secured. Not all of life changed, nor did all values and behavior, but the urge to break the law seemed to decrease in these instances,

although many others, more set in anti-social ways, did not respond so favorably.

Regardless of whether blocked opportunity underlies all, most, or only some delinquency, it is crucial for the lives of sublower-class people and, indeed, for all of us. There is no healthy place in our society for able-bodied adults who do not work regularly, for adolescents out of school and out of work, for those who do not have the basis for stable families, for children who grow up in an atmosphere of hopelessness, for neighborhoods of people and standards committed to either defeatism or illegitimate methods of survival. Large segments of our population are being pushed into what has been termed economic and social suicide.

Mention should be made of the special problems of young un-married parents. Girls can often return to school after the birth, but when boys are held responsible, they are apt to drop out and enter the labor market, poorly equipped. This is the beginning of another family whose children are likely to continue the weary round of problems.

These generalizations may not be able to rise to the task of con-veying the impact of the kinds of lives led and the tragic waste they include. Going to the neighborhoods, talking with the youngsters and workers, brings it all alive. A makeshift substitute would be to read descriptions such as that of the Hough Area in Cleveland,[1] of part of the Lower East Side in New York,[2] and of other areas where demonstration programs gathered this kind of information. Over and over again, the literature on unemployment emphasizes that the combination of masses of youth, lack of skills, and low educa-tional achievement, together with minority status, leads to meager occupational opportunities.

Added to these conditions is the set of attitudes and behaviors which develop among sublower-class teenagers. With poor occupa-tional models in the family and neighborhood, problems with au-thority, and the generally low expectations of them, the youngsters acquire unrealistic notions, poor work habits, insufficiently controlled impulses, and ineptness in finding and holding jobs. As an example

---

[1] Greater Cleveland Youth Service Planning Commission, Inc., *Community Action for Youth: A Summary*, Cleveland, March, 1963, especially pages 8 and 9.
[2] Mobilization for Youth, Inc., *op. cit.*

one group of boys was helped by an agency to get a job shovelling snow in a suburb. When they arrived, they had no shovels and had not thought to raise questions about the needed equipment in advance. Many of the youth, in talks with them, mentioned occupational goals which were high indeed, such as medicine and architecture, without much chance of attainment. In fact, they would often panic before impending interviews for quite modest kinds of jobs. In addition, there is the expectation at times of wages far above the going rates for their levels of competence and experience. Where racketeering and theft are common, the "fast buck" is a visible reality and has an impact on their readiness to do hard work for a modest reward. Simply to provide a job is not enough. Programs which open up new and better legitimate job opportunities must be supported by skilled services which deal with the attitudes and habits of the youth, to help them through the frustrations and crises which inevitably occur.

In view of the massive evidence of the unreadiness of sublowerclass youngsters for the middle-class occupational world, there is the temptation to label them as lacking in capacity, intelligence and talent, a gross misjudgment. In a study of a sample of 13,715 pupils dropping out of school in Maryland for the year ending June 30, 1961,[3] about half were found to be of average or above average mental ability. Dropouts are not identical with the sublower class nor with delinquents, but there is a large overlap. There is also a high probability that the various means used to measure mental and other abilities show results well below the potentials of the sublower class. We should not fall into the destructive trap of blaming a kind of person for characteristics which many other types of people would show if subject to the same conditions.

The dropout situation is a curious one. To refer again to the Maryland publication, a paper by Daniel Schreiber, Director, National Education Association Project on School Dropouts, indicates that thirty years ago the national rate was fifty percent, as against the current (1962) rate of thirty-five percent. With all the effort and publicity being devoted to dropouts, the rate will probably decrease further. Yet dropouts have become one of the most pressing

[3] Maryland Commission for Children and Youth, Governor's Conference on School Dropouts and Employment Problems of Youth, Baltimore, September 27, 1962, p. 1.

educational and general concerns. The reasons lie in economic and
social changes which have re-defined the status of the dropout.
Whereas in the past there was the tradition and actuality of the
self-made man, one who by energy, cleverness and drive was able
to go far without the benefit of much schooling, today education is
essential. It is *the* door to a better life economically and otherwise.
With the added forces of sublower-class and minority position ar-
rayed against him, the future becomes all but hopeless for the dropout. Many of them do not find any kind of job when they quit
school, and the long days of idleness, about which they may have
dreamed while "cooped-up" are not easy to fill legitimately. Duke,
the main character in Warren Miller's *The Cool World*,[4] makes
the point nicely when he says that during school it is not difficult
to find something to do, such as playing truant; during vacations it
is tough to fill time. The long-run implications are worse. There is
apt to be no respectable future. Frequently there is a history of
educational failure or backwardness so that the youngster's command of the 3R's is shaky. Lacking the ability to fill out an application form, unable to read instructions, and feeble in his skill in
common needed arithmetical processes, his field is narrowed to
the most unskilled jobs. Not only are there insufficient numbers of
these to meet the demand, but the unskilled, uneducated teenager
must compete with adult counterparts, who appeal more to employers because they are apt to be more stable.

In addition to figures presented in Chapter One, an article [5] in
*Look,* presented the following:

Almost a million youngsters under twenty are neither in school nor
working.
While only one fourteenth of the labor force, youth compose one
sixth of the unemployed.
The number of sixteen-year-olds increased by a million in a year.

The article quotes Secretary of Labor W. Willard Wirtz as stating that youth unemployment could become "one of the most explosive problems in the nation's history." It also quotes Chicago's
Commission on Youth Welfare as predicting that the number of
young people leaving school to work will reach three million in

---

[4] Warren Miller, *The Cool World* (Boston: Little, Brown & Co., 1959).
[5] Samuel Grafton, "The Tense Generation," *Look,* August 27, 1963, p. 22.

1970. Yet the jobs for which they might be eligible are not increasing. The article does not go into the class distribution of youth unemployment but we know that it hits the sublower class the hardest, especially those in minority groups.

In the related realms of education and work, an impressive array of ideas and programs has been developed. The Maryland document [6] describes some of those in schools, as do publications [7] of the New York City Youth Board. The demonstrations in several cities largely financed by the President's Committee on Juvenile Delinquency and Youth Crime are stressing the education-work theme in their plans. Three Chicago agencies, in cooperation with Chicago business and industry, the Commission on Youth Welfare, the Illinois State Employment Services, and the University of Chicago, presented an ambitious proposal [8] for a year's program for a thousand youth who are least employable. They were to apply for federal funds.

These are additions to what the agencies already do. Mobilization for Youth has a tremendous array of programs in these areas. And the aforementioned do not begin to include the number of agencies trying to mitigate the opportunity problem. A comprehensive list and description [9] of guidance, placement, pre-employment training, work experiences and conservation projects was prepared by Kohler and Freedman.

There is a broad range of specifics: (1) tutoring and places to study, (2) introduction of smaller classes and more guidance, (3) education directed more to what is currently meaningful to youth, (4) cooperation with industries and other businesses in providing training, apprenticeship and somewhat guided work experiences, (5) agency-administered enterprises which permit youth to try out various occupational activities, (6) paid responsibility to supervise recreation for younger children, (7) job placement in

---

[6] *Op. cit.*

[7] *A Statement of Guiding Principles of the Compulsory Education and Child Labor Laws* and *Report of Mayor's Conference on Youth and Work* (New York City Youth Board [New York, 1961]).

[8] *Basic Education, On-the-Job Training and Work Education* (Chicago Boys Clubs, Chicago Youth Centers and Chicago YMCA [Chicago, Feb. 23, 1963]), dittoed, third draft.

[9] Mary Conway Kohler and Marcia K. Freedman, *Youth in the World of Work,* Taconic Foundation (New York, October, 1962).

private businesses with agencies paying part of the wages, and many others. Indications are that most of these efforts are relatively successful in helping many to move from aimless "hanging" on the streets toward a more organized existence built on the framework of a legitimate job producing a regular income. It is probably too early for these innovations to have shed much light on their effects on delinquency, but impressions are encouraging.

Just as the streetworker cannot do his job effectively alone and needs these educational and work programs to help him provide roads to adulthood, so these newer programs need him if they are to reach the most difficult to educate, train and place in jobs. Without him, relying on schools, other institutions and forms of publicity to make contacts, the education-training-work projects may attract youth who are less alienated—and certainly they deserve opportunities too—but the hard core youngsters are apt to respond through someone they know well and trust. If they are members of a gang with which the worker is well established, supporting group dimensions can be utilized. The worker's familiarity on the streets is a great asset, particularly if the program to which he is trying to bring the youngsters is not in a school building. The latter often has negative connotations, although it need not always be an insuperable obstacle. Thus, again we see the streetworker as a link with vital resources.

Broader and more difficult questions must be faced about the constellation of education-work problems of sublower-class youth and the gratifying surge of services designed to meet them. Many of the latter are supported by special grants from foundations and government departments, with a time-limiting feature. This is true of the experiments largely supported by the President's Committee. The congressional hearings on these programs during the Spring of 1963 were not in a mood reassuring to their futures. The most successful ways to help youth need sifting out, but a tragic situation would develop if support were withdrawn while thousands of youngsters were being helped. Allowing for shifts in emphasis and methods as more is learned about how to do the job and economic and social conditions change, any gross curtailment just to economize would be disastrous. These programs should be ended only when the need for them ceases, i.e., school dropouts decrease substantially, the attitudes of sublower-class youth toward school im-

prove, and jobs with appealing futures open up for these youngsters in numbers related to the size of their population. The achievement of these conditions is nowhere on the horizon. Fortunately, minorities are awakening to their rights and they are apt to join others who want to see that young people are given the opportunity and legitimate wherewithal to live decently.

The costs of programs to help alienated youth are high. It is hard to know how they compare with the costs of police, courts, incarceration, and possible dependency on welfare funds for generations, because this is not a precise mathematical equation. While the cost of rehabilitation, for instance, can usually be ascertained, it is difficult to be certain that it will always accomplish the desired results and hence eliminate the need for the other monies. Cost-accounting has its uses, but also its severe limitations. Suppose that enormous sums are spent and only twenty percent of those served do not continue to be delinquent or dependent. Are these investments then wasted? What about the worth of each of the many in the twenty percent who now know a new and better life? What kind of accounting should we apply to them? Suppose only one person is genuinely helped—a rare occurrence—by a program. Is it wasted? Middle-class parents are ready to spend all they have on a child who needs expensive help. Why should the community do less?

The consequences engendered by the upward movement of sub-lower-class youth are not entirely clear-cut. Menial jobs in our society need doing, such as housework, cleaning and sweeping public buildings, garbage collection, and many others. The lower class has come in handy. If all of them become educated and skilled, who will perform these functions for the rest of us? What would happen if Negroes, Puerto Ricans and Mexican-Americans, among others, suddenly went back to their places of origin? The middle class would tremble and a new hierarchy would have to be developed fast. The tragedy has been that people have been locked in the cellar of our society without regard to their abilities and potentials. Some people as individuals may be more content with the simpler and generally less-appealing jobs but not whole races and ethnic groups. The time has come when we must be ready to accept as colleagues and more those we have regarded suitable as janitors. This presupposes a shift in relationships and power with-

out which the prevention of delinquency and the offering of more generous educational and job opportunities are superficial. This is where, unconsciously, alienated youth lead us.

To be more specific, capable sublower-class youngsters need much help with education to reach the professional and other levels where demand exceeds supply. In the settings in which they receive training, it is hoped that in whatever kind of work they do, they will be exposed to higher occupational levels.[10] This would be the case in a hospital but less so in a laundry. Bringing to life the realities of work with greater prestige and assisting with its essential preparation is vital. Who and how many succeed in rising to higher socio-economic levels should depend on individual capacities and efforts, not on the family, race, ethnic group and neighborhood into which the youth happen to be born. This is the American heritage but to achieve it will require revolutionary changes in our attitudes toward education, economics, housing, and, above all, toward people.

An intermediate level of objectives is jobs which call for some skill and training, but not college and even graduate school, as is true of many professions. Such middle-level jobs have been identified—auto mechanics, electrical work and numerous others. Those planning the training indicate that there are openings for youngsters on this level.

But there will still be a mass of young people entering the market without skills. For this hurdle there is no realistic solution in sight and the problem has not even been tackled comprehensively. While there are examples of industries ready to make adaptations to permit the employment of some sublower-class unskilled youth, the trend is strongly the other way. Instances are piling up on a vast scale of the elimination of unskilled jobs by automation. Furthermore, industry is committed to efficiency and profit, not to social welfare. If, as was said in connection with a training program at the Sears YMCA in Chicago, lower-class, minority and gang youngsters can be helped to function as well as or better than other young people do, why not hire them? But this does not tend to increase the total number of openings for unskilled youth. Where industry is highly automated, as in Detroit, the prognosis for em-

---

[10] Suggested to the writer by Dr. Catherine V. Richards.

ployment of sublower-class youth was gloomy indeed, during a year (1963) when the sale of automobiles was high. A similarly discouraging outlook existed in Cleveland and in other cities. We are in the strange situation which simultaneously includes increasing employment and unemployment. In a special message to Congress reported in the Chicago *Daily News,* February 14, 1963, President Kennedy was quoted as saying:

> "I have already proposed tax and other measures designed to quicken the pace of economic activity to increase the prospects for full employment. . . . But the rate of youth unemployment will still remain disproportionately high for some time unless other, more direct measures are adopted. Our young persons are caught in cross-currents of population growth and technological change which hold great danger as well as great promise."

The President posed the problem clearly and vividly. Even with the most optimistic expectations or hopes for prosperity, the outlook for deprived youth is dismal.

Elsewhere in the same message the President made specific proposals. A major one was a Youth Conservation Corps to improve forests and recreation areas which would provide training and work for 15,000 young people.[11] A second proposal would pay half the wages and related costs for work in local non-profit community services, such as hospitals, schools, parks and settlement houses, indicating that 40,000 young people would be so employed the first year. He also recommended that the Juvenile Delinquency Act (under which the President's Committee operates) should have its funds extended three years beyond the original three. Various other recommendations were made by the President, among them the National Service Corps, which, although not focused on the employment of lower-class youth, might benefit them through its services, and the upgrading of social work, educational and health programs. It is significant that in his discussion of delinquency the President said that the underlying "malady is a lack of opportunity."

Earmarked by the President for the two proposals to increase

---

[11] It was reassuring to read in the *Boston Globe,* September 15, 1963, that a Gallup Poll found that such camps were favored by eighty-nine percent, while only six percent regarded them as a "poor idea," with five percent having "no opinion." Few issues have received such decidedly favorable opinion.

employment for lower-class youth was $100,000,000, included in the 1964 budget recommendations. This is quite a sum, but it does not approach the appropriations for space, defense and foreign aid. We have underdeveloped segments of our own country, and it is hard to imagine any cause with a greater claim on our resources than the critical situation of so many of our youth. The crucial questions are rather whether funds will be made available by Congress, whether they will come quickly enough, whether they will be administered in a way which will take full account of the complexities in dealing with sublower-class youth, and whether they will be sufficient to encompass a mammoth problem.

There is a marked danger arising from the use of only a single explanation of delinquency, opportunity-blockage in this instance. The CCC of the Depression days worked with poverty-stricken youth, but this condition was general and the youth were not likely to be as deviant or sharply separated in their values as our present poor. If the selective process for the proposed Youth Conservation Corps is not handled thoughtfully, it could resemble some of the difficult housing projects in concentrating so much pathology in one place that healthier youth would not be able to set the tone and would cause the work of the staff to become formidable, if not impossible. The experience with the various work projects described earlier in this chapter argues strongly for providing services which will help the youth adjust to and benefit from the new work opportunities. Without such services, the casualties are apt to be heavy.

The President's youth program, which does not go far enough, has been called socialistic by some. This reaction to the extension of federal programs has been evident on many occasions when measures were under consideration to help the poor and others. Social Security is a good example, and it seems to be with us to stay. Youth unemployment is a massive problem with consequences which could reach calamitous proportions. The present dimensions and configurations of the opportunity problems of sublower-class youth are of too recent origin for their full impact to be felt. If adequate steps are not taken to solve them during the next few decades, the nation will experience pathology more pervasive, dangerous and expensive than it ever dreamed could exist. We would then have staggering numbers of adults who never knew what it

means to work regularly and be legitimately independent. What will happen to their children?

However many youth are employed by industry and agencies are that many to the good. Cities and states have important responsibilities. But only the federal government has the resources to meet problems of this enormity. If it does not respond to them, the future of the nation is dark.

## CHAPTER NINE

THE AMERICAN PEOPLE have repeatedly demonstrated their generosity and sense of responsibility when vividly confronted with catastrophes and human misery, wherever they exist. The failure to respond sufficiently to the legitimate rights of millions in our own sublower class has diverse origins, but lack of awareness of the

# Conclusion

extent and seriousness of the problems must be a large source of it. What else can excuse a congressional committee's criticism of Mobilization for Youth for spending too much per person served? [1] The objection was not that the program was poorly conceived or ineffective. It just cost too much. Do we apply this kind of cost-accounting to armaments, rockets and foreign aid?

It is sadly true that we tend to get aroused only by dramatic crises. Killings in gang fights, the murder of an innocent bystander, hit the headlines and ring bells. It is as though in the field of public health we waited for a large-scale epidemic of typhoid before taking vigorous and comprehensive action. Much is going on to cope with delinquency, but practically everywhere it is underfinanced, understaffed and poorly supported in other ways. Americans need to be better informed about all this, and the agencies who know the story so well should tell it more loudly and clearly. The mass media, which have not neglected delinquency, need to do much more about it. Officials and others in high positions need to recognize the problems and respond more to them; they have claims on all of us at least as great as those of roads and other things on which enormous sums are spent. Expressways enable middle-class people to go through lower-class areas so fast that they catch little hint of the poor conditions of living, frustration and hopelessness beyond the edges of the highways.

[1] *The New York Times,* April 27, 1963.

Delinquency is woven into the texture of our society. Seemingly unrelated acts have their effects. The stoning of a Negro's newly-purchased home in a previously all white neighborhood adds to the confinement of minorities to deteriorated, congested and deprived sections. The march on Washington in August, 1963, provided lift and hope, yet we are still in the infancy stage of solving these problems.

The automating of factories, worsening crowding of schools and many other such developments have their impact. Effective action requires basic social, economic and political change. Often unknowingly, and sometimes not, we are feeding the fires of poverty and delinquency on a scale with which agencies trying to control and prevent them cannot keep pace. Work with dropouts, with gangs and with youth in courts, can be and often is enormously helpful, but it cannot alone compete effectively with the gigantic maldistribution of income, good jobs, decent housing, political power and all the rest. We have our own underdeveloped areas. It is heartening that Americans are ready to do so much for such areas in distant countries, as indicated by Foreign Aid and the Peace Corps, but insufficient attention and resources are being devoted to our own underfed, ill-housed, uneducated and unskilled people, and to what needs to be done to help. The changes which we hope will occur in the poor will be possible only if changes occur in all of us, especially in our attitudes toward them.

While hopefully the large canvas of social, economic and political conditions is being repainted, the agencies working with delinquents must be better-supported and given much higher status, being among our most precious assets in preserving and enhancing human decency. The current step-child-like situation of many of them, especially those working on the streets, is not consistent with the level of strength and prestige essential for the size and complexity of their tasks.

There is a rising tide of social consciousness and sense of responsibility among college students. Work with delinquents is made-to-order for harnessing this hopeful energy in professions which serve them. Volunteers in sizable numbers are now tutoring sublower-class youngsters and helping in other ways. Important as is the contribution of volunteers, a large increase in highly trained professionals is essential in all the related fields. Adequate

financing would make it more possible to create conditions attractive enough to build whole careers with good futures in these fields.

The coordination among the diverse agencies has advanced but much remains to be done. No one type has primacy, and each needs the others. Again, adequate financing would free staff time for fuller coordination.

Population movement, whether from one part of a city to another or from the South to the North, has added to the lack of norms and the problems of social control. While the spirit and letter of American democracy fortunately do not permit the regulation of where people should live, all too little attention has been given to the grouping of families in housing projects, to shifts arising from urban renewal, and to longer distance migrations from the standpoint of the social conditions they create. If the many thousands of Negroes and some whites going to large Northern cities from the South had the benefit of accurate information about jobs, housing and other situations, some might go elsewhere or remain at home. Certainly it is damaging to them to be concentrated in large numbers in terrible slums. Restrictions of minorities to severely limited areas accentuates the congestion. We do not know how they would have been received in smaller Northern communities. Be that as it may, we need machinery for gathering and disseminating accurate information about population distribution in relation to living conditions and jobs. Certainly there need to be revisions of policies which determine the admissions to housing projects so that they do not continue to have so high a percentage of families with acute problems.

The confluence of the population explosion, minority tensions, increased unemployment of the unskilled and uneducated, concentration of deprived and frustrated people in limited areas of our large cities, and the feeling of hopelessness about the future, brooks no delay in the marshalling of far greater resources. Each day that goes by sees some youngsters being drawn more deeply into the delinquency mold, drinking, using dope, conceiving and bearing children, stealing cars, and all of the rest on the list. Some are moving into the stage where no known method may be able to reach them.

Perhaps the most terrible aspect of the situation is the way the present flows into the future. Teenage parents, struggling for a place for themselves, are not in a position to give their children the

attention and stability required for their healthy growth. The conditions which stimulated the delinquent adolescents to be what they are operate on their children. The phenomena of delinquency, crime, dependency and illegitimacy going through generations is not rare.

The interesting point has been made that there is a self-regenerating power in people. As an example, although the matriarchal pattern is so common in sublower-class families, succeeding generations will learn how to develop more balanced and satisfying family lives. There probably is profound truth in this view of human nature but regeneration must have some base in socio-economic conditions. The adult male cannot be breadwinner, loving husband and father, and bulwark of the family, if he is uneducated, unemployed, frustrated and defeated. Yet this is the route unwittingly prescribed for so many teenage boys today. The time to act is now.

A source of sustenance and pride in American history is that our people have somehow managed to find the wisdom and resources for meeting the tests of its great crises. Today's delinquency with all its accompanying problems is such a crisis. We can meet it effectively. What will history say of *us*?

# appendix a

Cities and Streetwork Agencies* Visited

1. Boston (Because of long experience in Boston, it was not necessary to visit as many agencies as in other cities.)
   Community Services Center, United South End Settlements
   YMCA
   Youth Activities Bureau
2. Chicago
   Chicago Commons
   Chicago Youth Centers
   Neighborhood Service Organization
   YMCA
   Youth Development Project—Boys' Club
3. Cleveland (Some cancelled because of snowstorm)
   Bell Center—Goodrich
   Division of Recreation
   League Park Center
   Mt. Pleasant Community Center
   Woodhill Housing Project
4. Detroit
   Neighborhood Service Organization
5. Los Angeles
   Group Guidance Section, Probation Department
   Neighborhod Youth Association
   Special Service for Groups
6. New York
   James Weldon Johnson Community Center
   Manhattanville Community Centers
   Mobilization for Youth
   New York City Youth Board

---

* Some of these agencies have branches, which were visited.

7. Philadelphia
    Crime Prevention Association
    Friends Neighborhood Guild
    United Neighbors Association
    Youth Conservation Services, Department of Welfare
8. San Francisco
    Hunters Point Boys Club
    Telegraph Neighborhood Association
    Youth for Service
9. Washington, D. C.
    District of Columbia Recreation Department

# **a**ppendix **b**

BOSTON UNIVERSITY SCHOOL OF SOCIAL WORK
264 Bay State Road, Boston 15, Massachusetts

STUDY OF GROUP WORK WITH STREET GROUPS

SAUL BERNSTEIN

*Questions or Issues*

1. What associational patterns among young people (anti-social)
   are you and your agency finding? Cohesive and highly organized gangs? Loose clusters? Are you working largely with the
   cohesive type of gang? Have changes been occurring in your
   community, such as from well-organized gangs toward looser
   clusters of members? If so, what are they? Are there reasonably consistent differences between girls' and boys' gangs? Are
   there social changes, such as a large in-migration of low status
   people, to which gang developments seem to be related?
2. The idea has been advanced that chances for success are increased when group cohesion is strong. Does this seem to be
   true of your experience? What implications does this hypothe-

sis have for work with small clusters of individuals? Does your goal then become that of stimulating group feeling in a larger number, or of using an approach very much like case work, or something else?

3. Is it the practice of your agency to form groups of anti-social and/or delinquent youngsters? If so, do they all tend to be of this type or do you include some non-deviant members? What guidelines do you use in deciding on the composition of such formed groups? Do they usually last? Other comments on this point?

4. What criteria seem sound for the selection of groups with which to work? As you look back on experiences with various groups, are there some which you now think should not have been selected for this type of service? If so, does this suggest further criteria for selection? What kinds of information tend to be available for a decision about whether to work with a specific gang and from what sources? Does this information tend to provide an adequate basis for the decision?

5. What were the characteristics of the groups with which you have had the greatest success? The least success? Does success or failure tend to apply to all or some or only a few members? Was there anything different or special about the way you worked with each of these categories? What seems to be the greatest obstacle to success in your work with gangs?

6. It has been stated that the most realistic goal in terms of expectations of achievement is constructive change in "public behavior," such as gang fights, group stealing and vandalism, and that the outlook is not so promising in relation to changes in "private behavior," such as the use of drugs, sex, etc. Is this position supported by your experience? Realistically, what success have you experienced in the improvement of interpersonal relations, and in helping the youngsters with education and jobs? What about the question as to whether changes in the group in the presence of the worker carry over to other situations?

7. What criteria does your agency use for decisions about the termination of work with a gang, assuming that the agency is in a position to make this decision? In your experience, has termination been applied to the whole group or to selected

members? What steps are taken to lead up to it? Is it customary to refer the group or individual to another agency? Is there any follow-up?

8. Does your agency make the worker available to the group for whatever amounts of time that may be needed or wanted, or does it limit this time (two periods per week in one instance)? What do you regard as the pros and cons of each approach?

9. Is it your agency's practice to focus only on the group members or to relate additionally to their families and the community?

10. Does your agency limit its services to group work or does it include others (casework, community organization, job placing, etc.)? In relation to what kinds of problems do you turn to other agencies? Is this cooperation reasonably successful? Are there services which gang members need which are not available in the community?

11. In what areas have you had good relationships with law enforcement agencies? Which have been the problem areas and what has been done about them?

12. Does your agency have psychiatric consultation? Under what conditions do you seek this help? Does he do treatment (of your members) as well as consultation? Do you refer group members to psychiatric agencies? If so, can you generalize about the results? Please comment on your experiences in turning to psychiatrists in connection with your work.

13. A. There has been much discussion of the importance of limited opportunities in relation to jobs and education as factors in delinquency. How does this position check with your experience and thinking?

    B. Does your agency attempt to help young people in these two areas: jobs and education? If so, what is done and how well do you think it is going?

14. Have you recently begun or are you contemplating experimentation with new approaches? If so, what are they?

15. Please comment on staff training needs in relation to what training opportunities are available. At which, if any, points do you see a need for increased training resources?

16. What are the value issues you see in work with anti-social young people?

# bibliography

Area Youth Work Committee, Health and Welfare Council, no title given, mimeographed, Philadelphia, July, 1960.

Austin, David M., "Goals for Gang Workers," *Social Work,* II, No. 4, October, 1957.

Bernstein, Saul, "Charting Group Progress," *Readings in Group Work,* Dorothea Sullivan, Editor, Association Press, 1952.

————, Kobrin, Solomon, *et al., Proceedings: Institute on Work with Youth in Conflict,* University of Illinois School of Social Work, 1959.

Blake, Mary E., *Youth Groups in Conflict,* Children's Bureau, Washington, D. C., 1958.

————, "Youth Workers and the Police," *Children,* September-October, 1961.

Bloch, H. and Niederhoffer, A., *The Gang.* New York: Philosophical Library, 1958.

Bordua, David J., "Delinquent Subcultures: Sociological Interpretations of Gang Delinquency," *The Annals,* American Academy of Political and Social Sciences, Philadelphia, November, 1961.

Brueckner, William H., "The Corner Group Worker as a Change Agent in the Life of the Group and Its Members," Chicago Commons Association. Paper presented to the Illinois Academy of Criminology, November 9, 1960.

Caplan, Nathan S. *et al., The Nature, Variety and Patterning of Street Club Work,* presented at meetings sponsored by the Youth Studies Center of the University of Southern California, Los Angeles, August 26, 1963.

Cartwright, Desmond S. and Lee, Ronal L., "Consulting with Detached Workers," University of Colorado. (Mimeographed, undated.)

Chicago Boys Clubs, Chicago Youth Centers, and Chicago YMCA, *Basic Education on the Job Training and Work Education,* dittoed, third draft, Chicago, February 23, 1963.

Children's Bureau, *Juvenile Delinquency References,* Washington, D. C., 1961.

Clague, Ewan, "Demographic Trends and Their Significance," Commissioner of Labor Statistics, U. S. Dept. of Labor, *The Changing Amer-*

*ican Population,* A Report of the Arden House Conference, 1962. p. 15.

Cloward, Richard A., "Social Problems, Social Definitions and Social Opportunities," unpublished, April, 1963.

Cloward, Richard A. and Ohlin, Lloyd E., *Delinquency and Opportunity.* Glencoe, Illinois: Free Press, 1960.

Cohen, Albert K., *Delinquent Boys.* Glencoe, Illinois: Free Press, 1955.

Collier, Al, Senior Deputy Probation Officer, Group Guidance Section, Los Angeles Probation Department, "Gang Information System— Analysis and Interpretation," undated.

Ephron, Lawrence R. and Piliavin, Irving, *A New Approach to Juvenile Delinquency,* Survey Research Center, University of California, Berkeley, California, 1962.

Freeman, Barry M., *Techniques of a Worker with a Corner Group of Boys,* Master's thesis. Available at Nursing-Social Work Library, Boston University, 1956.

Frey, Louise and Meyer, Marguerite. *Exploration and Working Agreement in Two Social Work Methods.* Available in Boston University Nursing-Social Work Library, 1962. (Mimeographed.)

Fyvel, T. R., *The Trouble-makers.* New York: Shocken Books, 1961-62.

Gandy, John M., "Preventive Work with Street Corner Groups: The Hyde Park Youth Project, Chicago," *The Annals,* American Academy of Political and Social Sciences, Philadelphia, March, 1959.

Goodman, Paul, *Growing Up Absurd.* New York: Vintage Books, 1962.

Grafton, Samuel, "The Tense Generation," *Look,* August 27, 1963.

Greater Cleveland Youth Service Planning Commission, Inc., *Community Action for Youth: A Summary,* Cleveland, March, 1963.

Herzog, Elizabeth, "Some Assumptions about the Poor," *Social Service Review* (December, 1963).

————, *Some Guidelines for Evaluative Research,* Children's Bureau, 1959.

Hollingshead, August B. and Redlich, Frederick C., *Social Class and Mental Illness,* New York: John Wiley & Sons, 1958.

Hoult, Thomas F. and Mayer, Albert J., *The Population Revolution in Detroit,* Detroit: Institute for Regional and Urban Studies, Wayne State University, 1963.

Kobrin, Solomon and Baittle, Brahm, *Sociological and Psychiatric Aspects of a Street Corner Group,* Children's Bureau, 1962.

Kohler, Mary Conway and Freedman, Marcia K., *Youth in the World of Work.* New York: Taconic Foundation, October, 1962.

Kolodny, Ralph, "Research Planning and Group Work Practice," *Mental Hygiene,* XXXXII, No. 1, January, 1958.

Kvaraceus, William C. and Miller, Walter B., *Delinquent Behavior: Culture and the Individual,* National Education Association, Washington, D. C., 1959.

Lerman, Paul, "Group Work with Youth in Conflict," *Social Work,* III, No. 4, October, 1958.

Lerner, Max, *America as a Civilization.* New York: Simon & Schuster, 1957.

Los Angeles County Probation Department and Youth Studies Center, University of Southern California, *Progress Report, Study of Delinquent Gangs,* July 1, 1961—June 30, 1962.

Margulies, Martin, *Measuring Changes in the Behavior and Attitudes of Street Corner Groups towards an Agency with a Detached Worker Service,* Master's Thesis, Boston University School of Social Work, 1959.

Martin, John H., "Social-Cultural Differences: Barriers in Casework with Delinquents," *Social Work,* II, No. 3, July, 1957.

Maryland Commission for Children and Youth, *Governor's Conference on School Dropouts and Employment Problems of Youth,* Baltimore, September 27, 1962. p. 1.

Mattick, Hans W. and Caplan, Nathan S., *Chicago Youth Development Project: Street Work, Community Organization and Research,* April 1, 1962.

Mattick, Hans W. and Caplan, Nathan S. *Stake Animals, Loud Talking and Leadership in Do-Nothing and Do-Something Situations,* presented at meetings sponsored by the Youth Studies Center of the University of Southern California, August 25, 1963.

Miller, Walter B., *City Gangs:* "A Report on the Mid-city Delinquency Study," *Boston University School of Social Work Journal,* I, January, 1963.

————, "Lower Class Culture as a Generating Milieu of Gang Delinquency," *Journal of Social Issues,* XIV, No. 3, 1958.

————, "Preventive Work with Street Corner Groups," *The Annals,* American Academy of Political and Social Sciences, Philadelphia, March, 1959.

————, "The Impact of a 'Total-Community' Delinquency Control Project," *Social Problems,* X, No. 2, Fall, 1962.

Miller, Warren, *The Cool World.* Boston: Little, Brown & Co., 1959.

Mobilization for Youth, Inc., *A Proposal for the Prevention and Control of Delinquency by Expanding Opportunities,* Mobilization for Youth, New York, August, 1962.

National Council on Crime and Delinquency, *Current Projects in the Prevention, Control and Treatment of Delinquency*, Spring, 1962.

Neighborhood Youth Association, *Changing the Behavior of Hostile Delinquency Prone Adolescents*, Los Angeles, 1960. Follow-up study, 1962.

New York City Youth Board, *A Statement of Guiding Principles of the Compulsory Education and Child Labor Laws*, New York, 1961, and *Report of Mayor's Conference on Youth and Work*, New York, 1961.

————, *New Directions in Delinquency Prevention*, 1947-57.

————, *Reaching the Teen Age Addict: A Study of Street Club Work with a Group of Adolescent Users*, New York, undated.

————, *Reaching the Fighting Gang*, 1960.

————, *Reaching the Unreached*, 1952.

————, *Teen Age Gangs*, 1957.

Ottawa Youth Services Bureau, Ottawa Welfare Council, *Identifying and Controlling Delinquent Groups of Boys*, Ottawa, Canada, 1963.

Peck, Harris and Bellsmith, Virginia, *Treatment of the Delinquent Adolescent*, Family Service Association of America, New York, 1947.

Pinamonti, Guido, *Special Social Group Work Services: A Study of the Role Which Voluntary Community Chest Funds Have in Support of this Service in the Los Angeles Area*, Metropolitan Recreation and Youth Services Council, Los Angeles, October, 1962.

Redl, Fritz, *The Aggressive Child*. Glencoe, Illinois: Free Press, 1957.

Richards, Catherine V., "Finding a Focus for Work with Hostile Youth Groups," *Social Work with Groups*, 1958.

Roth, Norman R., *Reaching the Hard-to-Reach, A Report of the Huntington-Gifford Project on Hard to Reach Youth*. Huntington Family Centers, Syracuse, N. Y., 1961.

Salisbury, Harrison E. *The Shook-Up Generation*. Greenwich, Connecticut: Crest Book, Fawcett Publications, 1958.

Samuels, Gertrude, "Death of a Youth Worker," *Saturday Evening Post*, April 4, 1963.

Short, James F., Jr. and Strodbeck, Fred L., *The Response of Gang Leaders to Status Threats: An Observation on Group Process and Delinquent Behavior*, revision of a paper read at the annual meeting of the American Sociological Association, August, 1961, mimeographed.

Silberman, Charles E., "The City and the Negro," *Fortune*, March, 1962.

Simcox, Beatrice and Kaufman, Irving, *Character Disorders in Parents*

*of Delinquents,* Family Service Association of America, New York, 1959.

Spergel, Irving, "An Exploratory Research in Delinquent Subcultures," *Social Service Review,* XXXV, No. 1, March, 1961.

———, *Exploring Delinquent Subcultures,* mimeographed, undated.

Thrasher, Frederick M.; *The Gang,* Chicago: University of Chicago Press, 1927.

Welfare Council of Metropolitan Chicago, *Breaking through Barriers,* 1960.

Wilson, Gertrude and Ryland, Gladys, *Social Group Work Practice.* Boston: Houghton Mifflin Company, 1949.

Witmer, Helen L. and Tufts, Edith, *The Effectiveness of Delinquency Prevention Programs,* Children's Bureau, 1954.

Yablonsky, Lewis, *The Violent Gang.* New York: Macmillan Company, 1962.